Day T

GETAWAYS LESS THAN TWO HOURS AWAY

SHIFRA STEIN'S **DAYTRIPS**®

FROM **NASHVILLE**

Fifth Edition

Susan Chappell

The Globe Pequot Press

GUILFORD, CONNECTICUT

ISSN 1538-6767
ISBN 0-7627-2972-4

Manufactured in the United States of America
Fifth Edition/First Printing

To Lindsay, Anna, and Lily,
for making home such a sweet place
to come back to

ILLINOIS

TENNESSEE

ALABAMA

0   10   20   30 miles

Ohio River

45

Metropolis
Paducah
Smithland
453
Kuttawa
Old Kuttawa
Grand Rivers
24
68
Land Between the Lakes
Aurora
Golden Pond
The Trace
139
24
68
Cadiz
41A
Oak Grove
Fort Campbell
79
Clarksville
Dover
12
41A
49
Ashland City
12
White Bluff
Joelton
Madison
Kingston Springs

Western Kentucky Parkway

70

431

Green River Parkway

Bowling Green
31W
South Union
31W
Russellville
68
73
65
80
79
431
Franklin
52
Adams
41
Springfield
76
431
Gallatin
Goodlettsville
109
Hendersonville
The Hermitage

Nashville

Briley Parkway

Opryland U.S.A.
231
Smyrna

Camden
Waverly
70
Dickson
Brentwood
Hurricane Mills
46 Bon Aqua
100
96
Franklin
41
24
Mu
Lyles
40
48
Leipers Fork
Spring Hill
College Grove
Christiana
Bell Buc
Wildersville
Natchez Trace State Resort Park and Forest
Tennessee River
Centerville
Duck River
Williamsport
31
Columbia
50
50
31A
41A
269
100
48
Linden
Hohenwald
43
373
65
Culleoka
Lewisburg
Shelbyville
82
20
Summertown
50
Ethridge
31
231
431
231
Ly
Mulberi
64
64
Natchez Trace Parkway
Lawrenceburg
Pulaski
Fayetteville
Kelso
Adamsville
Crump
22
Savannah
Shiloh
128
142
Pickwick Dam
57
Counce
231
431

72
565
Huntsville

Decatur

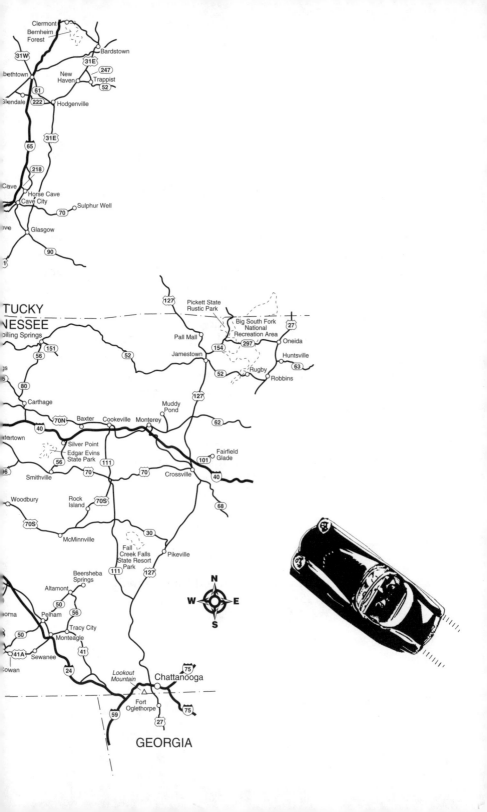

Help Us Keep This Guide Up to Date

Every effort has been made by the author and editors to make this guide as accurate and useful as possible. Many things, however, can change after a guide is published—establishments close, phone numbers change, facilities come under new management, etc.

We would love to hear from you concerning your experiences with this guide and how you feel it could be made better and be kept up-to-date. While we may not be able to respond to all comments and suggestions, we'll take them to heart and we'll make certain to share them with the author. Please send your comments and suggestions to the following address:

The Globe Pequot Press
Reader Response/Editorial Department
P.O. Box 480
Guilford, CT 06437

Or you may e-mail us at:
editorial@GlobePequot.com

Thanks for your input, and happy travels!

Contents

Preface

The state of Tennessee conjures up immediate images for most people. Country music certainly can be found at the top of many lists, but so can the unspoiled land that makes up this long narrow state. From the flatlands of Western Tennessee to the mountainous east, the state is as varied in land as it is in people.

Because of Nashville's unique location in the middle of the state, day-trippers can head north into Kentucky or south to Alabama in an hour's time. And in just two hours, travelers can even reach Georgia—finding both big cities and rural towns on the way.

Take to the road to explore a cave, ride a ferry, visit a national military park, tour a distillery, enjoy the wonder of space, watch wildlife, hang-glide, swim, canoe, shop, and eat—all within driving distance of home.

One thing that sets this area apart from the rest of the country is the prominence of Civil War history. Tennessee is second only to Virginia in the number of Civil War sites, a designation residents maintain with pride. The Commonwealth of Kentucky also amassed a wealth of Civil War history, supplying troops to both the Union and the Confederacy. And war leaders Abraham Lincoln and Jefferson Davis both hailed from the state.

Then there are music and horses. Tennessee is home to the Grand Ole Opry and the country music recording industry, and a slew of artists are based in the Middle Tennessee area. Kentucky's musical roots revolve around bluegrass, whose basic form was created by the late Kentuckian Bill Monroe in the 1940s.

The Tennessee walking horse is a world-class breed known for its rhythmic, gliding gait. And Kentucky, with its abundant horse farms and racetracks, is known as one of the best breeding grounds for Standardbreds and Thoroughbreds in the world.

Other highlights in this part of the country are that the folks are friendly, the food is "down home," and the scenery is splendid. Southerners are known for spinning a good yarn, so don't be shy about striking up a conversation with those you meet on your way. Most likely they'll be glad to impart whatever trivia or knowledge they have that will make your travels even more enjoyable. If you haven't explored the region lying within two hours or so of Nashville, you will be delighted with what you find. Whatever road you choose, you're sure to bring back memories that will fill your life's travelogue.

Travel Tips

Carry a Road Map

A road map is always a good idea if you're heading out for a drive. We have included directions for each day trip, but some travelers may opt for a different route. Most state departments of transportation provide free state maps, or you can purchase them at most service stations and bookstores. A couple of companies make a combined Tennessee/Kentucky map, a handy aid for some of the day trips in this book.

Follow the Rules of the Road

Since this book takes in more than one state, highway rules and regulations will vary. Be advised that Tennessee, Kentucky, and Alabama have state seat-belt laws. Play it safe and buckle up.

The Tennessee Department of Transportation has cycling maps for five different bike routes across the state if you happen to like riding a two-wheeler. An approved bicycle helmet is a must for cyclists and required by law for children under twelve on state highways. Call the Department of Transportation, (615) 253-2422, for the "Cycling Tennessee's Highways" packets.

Beware of Time Changes

On some day trips from Nashville, travelers will cross into a different time zone. Parts of Eastern Kentucky and Tennessee lie in the eastern time zone, which is an hour later than the central time zone. Be aware of the change in planning your travels.

View Fall Foliage

Both Tennessee and Kentucky are breathtaking during autumn. The foliage peaks somewhere between mid-September and October in both states. To find out where the peak color is in Kentucky, call (800) 225-TRIP or visit www.kentuckytourism.com. Tennessee offers a Fall Color Hotline that gives callers an updated status report on the state's changing foliage and events that celebrate the season. Peak areas are listed in a prerecorded message (updated each week beginning in mid-September and running through mid-November). Call (800) 697-4200 for the latest on the changing leaves.

Watch Out for Wild Animals

As in many states, various wild animals living in this travel area can pose a driving hazard. Keep your eye out for deer, raccoons, opossums, and miscellaneous livestock. Woods border many of Tennessee's and Kentucky's rural roads, so the likelihood of deer crossing the road is a real threat.

Sleep Away from Home

This book lists many bed-and-breakfasts in case you'd rather spend a little more time away from home. While many cities and towns have hotels/motels, a night in a B&B can add so much more to a trip. The majority of bed-and-breakfasts are family homes, run by people who are genuinely interested in getting to know their guests and making their stay an enjoyable one. B&Bs can vary from a rustic log cabin to a luxurious European-style inn.

Brochures are available from the Tennessee Bed & Breakfast Innkeepers Association. Call (800) 820-8144 or see www.tennessee -inns.com.

For B&Bs in Alabama, write the Bed and Breakfast Association of Alabama, P.O. Box 707, Montgomery, AL 36101; dial (800) 340-4074; or see www.bedandbreakfastalabama.com. The Bed & Breakfast Association of Kentucky is located at 1026 Russell Street, Covington, KY 41011. Call (800) 292-2632 or see www.kentuckybb.com.

Check Interesting Web Sites

If you have access to the Internet, you can find descriptions of more than 1,000 different bed-and-breakfasts across the country at www.bbonline.com. The official Tennessee state tourism Web site, at www.tnvacation.com, has all kinds of interesting information as well.

A Note about Tennessee State Parks and Resorts

Some of Tennessee's state parks and resorts are open on a limited schedule. If you are planning a trip that involves any state park facility, make sure you call ahead for hours.

Use This Travel Guide

Highway designations: Federal highways are designated US. State routes are indicated by TN for Tennessee, KY for Kentucky, AL for Alabama, and GA for Georgia.

Hours: Hours of operation have been omitted because they are subject to frequent changes. Instead, addresses and phone numbers appear for obtaining up-to-date information.

Restaurants: Restaurant prices are designated as $$$ (expensive; $15 and up for an entree), $$ (moderate; $5–$15), and $ (inexpensive; $5 and under).

Accommodations: Room prices are designated as $$$ (expensive; over $100 for a standard room), $$ (moderate; $50–$100), and $ (inexpensive; under $50).

Credit cards are accepted unless noted otherwise.

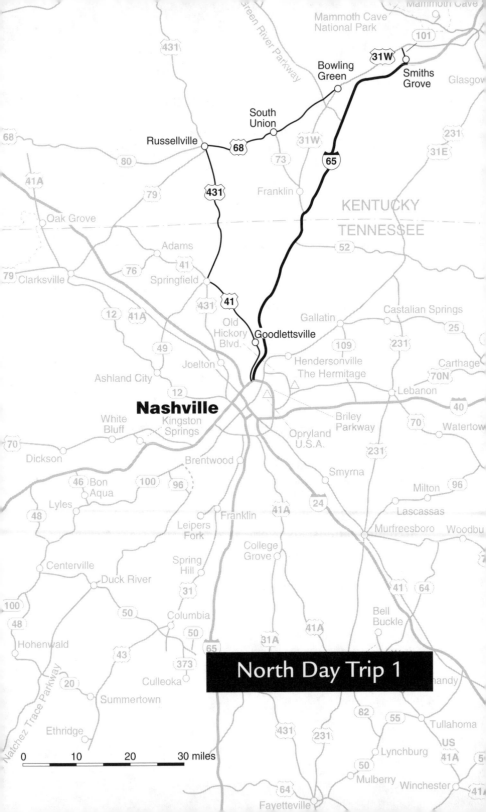

North Day Trip 1

GOODLETTSVILLE

About 12 miles north of Nashville on I–65 north or out Dickerson Pike (US–41 north) lies the small community of Goodlettsville. The town's close proximity to Nashville affords its 12,500 rural residents easy access to the big city.

WHERE TO GO

Bowen Plantation House. Located opposite Mansker's Station fort, it is said to be the oldest standing brick structure in Middle Tennessee. A good example of Federal-style architecture, the house was restored in 1976 and is listed on the National Register of Historic Places. Visitors can take guided tours led by interpreters dressed in period clothing. Each May the Eighteenth-Century Colonial Fair brings together craftsmen displaying reproductions of eighteenth-century goods, living-history reenacters, period food, and enjoyable music (see "Festivals and Celebrations"). Open daily; call for hours. Fee. (615) 859–3678.

   Historic Mansker's Station Frontier Life Center. 705 Caldwell Drive. Get off I–65 at exit 97 or take US–41 to Long Hollow Pike, turn right on Caldwell Drive, and continue until you see Moss-Wright Park.

   Mansker's Station is an authentic reproduction of the frontier fort built by Kasper Mansker in 1779. Three family cabins, two blockhouses, a tool shop workroom, and a blacksmith's shop have been reproduced to show what life was like in the early days. Plus,

1

"living-history" demonstrations from the eighteenth century take place throughout the year and give visitors an even deeper appreciation of pioneer life. Guided tours last about an hour. Open daily March through December. Fee. (615) 859-3678; http://manskers.historicalifestyles.com.

Long Hollow Winery & Vineyards. 665 Long Hollow Pike. Get off I-65 at exit 97, and turn east toward Gallatin. The winery is a mile ahead on the right. Long Hollow Winery is owned by Grand Ole Opry star Stu Phillips and his wife, Aldona. The winery, which opened in 2000, specializes in dry, semisweet, and sweet red and white wines, with names like Hush, Scarlet, and Shackle Island. The building is based on a monastery that Phillips visited as a youngster, with a gift shop adjacent to the tasting room. Complimentary wine tastings are offered daily, and personalized tours and concerts are available for large groups and special occasions by appointment. Open daily. (615) 859-5559; www.longhollowwinery.com.

RUSSELLVILLE

To get to Russellville from Goodlettsville, head north on US-41 until you reach Springfield. Just outside Springfield, turn right onto US-431 and drive north for 24 miles to this quaint county seat.

Russellville has one of the largest historic districts for its size in the Commonwealth of Kentucky. Kentucky is one of four states still known as a commonwealth, which was the designation it chose after separating from Virginia in 1792 (the term then was synonymous with "state"). Russellville also boasts the bank where the Jesse James Gang staged its first robbery in 1858 and the building where delegates from forty-three Kentucky counties decided on the state's secession from the Union. If you're shopping for antiques, you'll find several places to browse. October brings the annual Tobacco Festival, too. (See "Festivals and Celebrations.")

WHERE TO GO

Logan County Chamber of Commerce. 116 South Main Street. Stop by for more information on Russellville and the surrounding area. Visitors can take a walking tour that passes by more than forty antebellum homes, ten of which have historical markers. Open Monday through Friday. (270) 726-2206; www.loganchamber.com.

The Bibb House Museum. 183 West Eighth Street. This large Greek Revival home belonged to Major Richard Bibb, an officer in the American Revolution and an abolitionist who freed more than half of his slaves in 1829 and provided for their safe passage back to Liberia. Visitors can see antebellum furnishings, antiques, primitive tools, and implements. These contrast with the slave quarters and kitchen, which are also on view. Open May through December, Tuesday through Saturday, or by appointment. Fee. (270) 726-3190.

WHERE TO STAY AND EAT

Holly Tree Bed and Breakfast. 434 Maple Lane. Two upstairs guest rooms with private baths are what travelers will find at this historic brick home. The property, which is situated on a large lot, was built in 1817 and added onto in the 1850s. A full breakfast is available in the morning and varies according to the proprietor's whim. Dinner is offered by reservation only. The renovated home also has a pool and double porches. $$. (270) 725-8865.

The Log House. 2139 Franklin Road. This 8,000-square foot, two-story log home offers four guest rooms, all with private baths. Two of the rooms have working fireplaces and access to a screened-in porch. Breakfast brings on taste-tempting dishes such as eggs Benedict and huevos rancheros. There's a greenhouse with hot tub and a swimming pool, and the home, which is owned by a well-known textile designer, is accented with antiques and one-of-a-kind collectibles. Children are welcome. $$. (270) 726-8483; www.theloghousebandb.com.

The Washington House Bed and Breakfast. 283 West Ninth Street. Typical of the historic homes here, Washington House is a restored 1824 house, furnished in antiques, many of which are for sale. It is also the former home of John Whiting Washington, the third cousin of President George Washington. Two rooms and a suite, all with private baths, accommodate guests. Both a continental and full breakfast are available, and lunches and brunch are offered with advance reservations. $$. (866) 850-9282 or (270) 726-1240; www.bbonline.com/ky/washington.

SOUTH UNION

From Russellville, turn east on US-68/KY-80 and continue for 15 miles until you reach South Union. If you want to bypass Russellville, you can hop on I-65 north from Goodlettsville and get off at exit 20, then take the William Natcher Parkway to exit 5. Turn west then on US-68/KY-80, and South Union will be 10 miles up on the right.

WHERE TO GO

Shaker Museum at South Union. US-68/KY-80. Here visitors can relive the unique religious lifestyle of the Shakers in one of the seven remaining colonies still open to the public. (Another larger Shaker community is also located in Kentucky at Pleasant Hill, which is approximately 190 miles from Nashville.)

Established in 1807 and disbanded over a century later in 1922, Shakertown at South Union was one of nineteen Shaker villages in the United States. This particular colony became known for its handmade silk, and the community survived by selling packaged garden seeds and fruit preserves for many years.

The Shakers believed in simplicity and perfection, which is evident in the baskets, silk, and wooden tools and furnishings on display in the three-story Shaker-style building called the Centre House. Throughout the year this museum offers workshops, lectures, and demonstrations. There are also special annual events, including a Summer Shaker Festival in June (see "Festivals and Celebrations"). Open daily March 1 through the end of November. Fee. (270) 542-4167 or (800) 811-8379; www.shakermuseum.com.

WHERE TO STAY

The Shaker Tavern. KY-73 south (off US-68/KY-80, about 1½ miles from Shakertown). This bed and breakfast offers six guest rooms, some with detached private baths and one with a bath in the room, all decorated in Victorian-style antiques. It's a convenient place to stay if you're visiting Shakertown. Open year-round. $-$$. (270) 542-6801 or (800) 929-8701.

BOWLING GREEN

From South Union, Bowling Green is just 10 miles east on US–68/KY–80. Kentucky's fifth-largest city was also its Confederate capital during the Civil War. You can take a driving tour of war sites, aided by a brochure to explain their significance. Today the community carries two distinctions—it is known as the "Home of the Corvette" because it houses the world's only National Corvette Museum and Chevrolet Corvette plant, and it boasts the 200-acre campus of Western Kentucky University, which schools 15,000 students.

WHERE TO GO

Walking tours. To get a taste of Bowling Green, take a walking tour through one of the city's six historic districts. Both commercial and

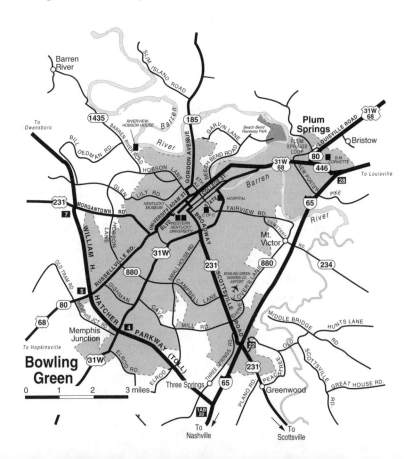

residential areas are dotted with structures built between 1860 and 1940 in various architectural styles, and all of the buildings within these districts are on the National Register of Historic Places. Stop by the Landmark Association at 912½ State Street for a brochure to guide you on your walk, or contact the Bowling Green Area Convention and Visitors Bureau, 352 Three Springs Road, Bowling Green, KY 42104. (207) 782-0800 or (800) 326-7465; www.bg.ky.net/tourism.

Capitol Arts Center. 416 East Main Street. Bowling Green's old Capitol Theatre, in the heart of downtown, has been renovated into a community arts center that features plays, dance, films, and other performances. Houchens Art Gallery and the Mezzanine Gallery also are housed in the 1939 Art Deco building, which sits directly across from Fountain Square Park, the focus of downtown Bowling Green since it was donated to the county for public use in 1978. For information on the current season, call (270) 782-2787 or (877) 694-2787; www.capitolarts.com.

General Motors Corvette Plant. 600 Corvette Drive. If you're traveling I-65, take exit 28, turn right at the first light onto Corvette Drive, and then make another right and follow the signs. GM relocated the only Corvette plant in the world to Bowling Green in 1981, and it became one of the largest tourist attractions in the state. The factory also produces the Cadillac XLR Roadster. Public tours are offered twice daily, Monday through Friday. Call ahead to check the status of plant tours, which can vary throughout the year. The National Corvette Homecoming is held the first weekend of June, featuring an array of activities revolving around the sports car (see "Festivals and Celebrations"). (270) 745-8419; www.bowling greenassemblyplant.com.

The Kentucky Museum and Library. Off Kentucky Street, Western Kentucky University campus. The Kentucky Museum has been documenting Kentucky's heritage since 1939, with three floors of galleries exhibiting a wide variety of artifacts. Contemporary art shows are also held here, and the library has a collection of published works, manuscripts, and folklife materials. The Felts Log House, located on the museum grounds, gives visitors a glimpse of life in the 1830s. Open weekends, May through October. Fee. (270) 745-2592.

Lost River Cave and Valley. US–31W and Cave Mill Road. This unusual cave is said to have the shortest, deepest river in the world flowing through it, according to "Ripley's Believe It or Not." The river measures 437 feet deep and runs only 350 feet before disappearing into one of the largest cave entrances in the eastern United States. The cave was discovered more than 10,000 years ago by Native Americans, and it was a place where both Union and Confederate soldiers camped during the Civil War.

It has been used as a mill and a distillery, and it was even an underground nightclub from the 1930s to the 1950s. The Butterfly Garden displays a wide array of the winged creatures native to the Bluegrass State, and more than fifty species of trees and plants can be seen from the valley's nature trail. Tours are offered daily, year-round, from 10:00 A.M. to 4:00 P.M., and include a boat tour into the cave. Fee. (270) 393-0077; www.lostrivercave.com.

National Corvette Museum. 350 Corvette Drive. This 68,000-square-foot museum showcases more than fifty Chevrolet Corvettes, including both one-of-a-kind and prototype models. In addition, there are racing and performance exhibits and hands-on educational opportunities. The Chevrolet Theater shows a Corvette Assembly Plant production film. A large gift shop carries all types of 'Vette memorabilia, and the museum is available for private parties and weddings. Open daily. Fee. (270) 781-7973; www.corvettemuseum.com.

Riverview at Hobson Grove Park. 1100 West Main Avenue. This stately three-story home, which sits up on a hill overlooking the park and the Barren River, is an ongoing restoration site, filled with period furnishings and artifacts dating from 1860 to 1890.

A beautiful Italianate design, the residence was used to store Confederate ammunition during the Civil War. Visitors can enjoy the Servant Life Tours, which are offered the third Saturday of each month. Call about special evening candlelight tours during December. The tours give the servants' perspective about what life was like then. Open Tuesday through Sunday; closed the Saturday before Christmas through January 31. Fee. (270) 843-5565; www.bgky.org/riverview.htm.

WHERE TO SHOP

Jackson's Orchard and Nursery. Slim Island Road (off Route 185). An orchard for more than eighty years, this 193-acre farm provides a pleasant stop away from the city. Summer peaches, fall apples, plums, cider, pumpkins, apple butter, and preserves are available for purchase. Pick the fruits yourself or buy them already plucked in the orchard gift shop. Open Monday through Saturday from mid-April through August; daily from September through November. (270) 781-5303.

WHERE TO EAT

Beijing Restaurant. 1951 Scottsville Road. This restaurant, with an unusual exterior that resembles a steamboat, has a varied menu of mostly Szechuan and Mandarin Chinese dishes. There are lunch specials, a full bar, and a Sunday lunch buffet. Open daily. $-$$. (270) 842-2288.

440 Main Restaurant. 440 East Main Street. The restored historic building overlooking Fountain Square Park makes a pleasant place to sample seafood, pasta, and other creative specialties. This place is also known for its award-winning wine list, hand-carved steaks, and New Orleans cuisine. Open for dinner Monday through Saturday. $$-$$$. (270) 793-0450; www.440main.com.

Hops Grill & Bar. 2945 Scottsville Road. This Florida-based eatery serves up steaks, prime rib, pasta, fresh seafood (flown in from the Sunshine State), salads, and burgers. The on-site microbrewery churns out several different beers to complement meals. Open daily for lunch and dinner. Children's menu. $$. (270) 781-1101.

Mariah's. 801 State Street. Located about a block from the downtown square, the Mariah Moore House is now a popular restaurant that opened in 1979. A stunning antique bar and outdoor terrace complement the historic 1818 home. Diners can choose from among salads, wood-fired pizzas, sandwiches, and a satisfying selection of pasta, chicken, and steak offerings. Open for lunch and dinner daily. $-$$. (270) 842-6878.

The Parakeet Cafe. 1129 College Street. Dine on fresh trout, salmon, chops, and other grilled items at this cozy eatery, which revamps its menu every six weeks. Open for dinner Monday through Saturday. $$-$$$. (270) 781-1538.

Riley's Bakery. 819 US-31W Bypass. A trip to Bowling Green wouldn't be complete without stopping at Riley's. This full-line bakery has been catering to the city's residents for more than sixty years. Specialties include salt-rising bread, brownies, Hungarian coffee cakes, and cream horns. Open Monday through Saturday. $-$$; credit cards not accepted. (270) 842-7636.

WHERE TO STAY

Bowling Green offers an abundance of places to stay. For more information about accommodations in the area, call the Bowling Green-Warren County Tourist and Convention Commission at (270) 782-0800.

Walnut Lawn Bed and Breakfast. 1800 Morgantown Road. Situated on the outskirts of the city, but close enough for easy access, this elegant restored home has been in the proprietor's family for more than one hundred years. Stroll the gardens or sit in one of the antiques-filled rooms. Four guest rooms (three of which have private baths) are decorated with vintage ladies' hats and shoes, and a continental breakfast is offered. Nonsmokers only; reservations a must. $$; credit cards not accepted. (270) 781-7255.

SMITHS GROVE

Get back on I-65 and head north to exit 38. Smiths Grove sits on the Louisville/Nashville railroad line, which contributed to its growth between 1859 and the 1920s. The peaceful community of about 750 is a mecca for antiques shoppers. The annual Smiths Grove Antique Festivals in May and October bring in dealers from five states to the small town (see "Festivals and Celebrations").

WHERE TO SHOP

Nine unique antiques stores line the streets of the Smiths Grove Historic District, attracting those looking for period furniture, linens, glassware, lamps, dolls, and collectibles. Stop by Wanda's (270-563-6444) or Wright House Antiques (270-563-9430) to get your shopping started.

WHERE TO STAY

Victorian House Bed and Breakfast. 110 North Main Street. This 1875 brick home sits on two acres right in the heart of Smiths Grove. The innkeepers have restored it to reflect the Victorian era and offer four rooms with private baths. The guest quarters are decorated with Victorian-style wallpaper and furnished with antiques and reproductions. A full country breakfast is on tap in the morning. A Victorian Day Spa on the premises offers massages, facials, manicures, and pedicures, and guests can make appointments for spa services. Catering facilities are also available. $$. (270) 563–9403; www.bbonline.com/ky/victorian.

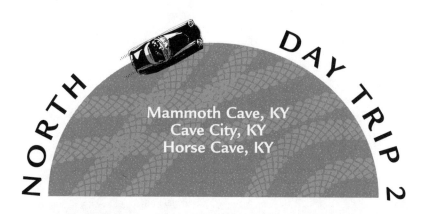
MAMMOTH CAVE

The best reason to head to Kentucky's "Cave Country" is to experience the wonder of Mammoth Cave, said to be the longest known cave system in the world. If you have kids in tow, there are many different attractions reminiscent of the 1950s that the little ones will get a kick out of. This part of Kentucky is on central time.

WHERE TO GO

Mammoth Cave National Park. Exit I-65 at Cave City (exit 53), and the park is 10 miles west on KY-70. There's a reason this Kentucky cavern is called "mammoth," with more than 300 miles of known cave passageways, and the park itself has some 52,000 acres of bluffs and forests. In addition, there are 70 miles of hiking trails and 30 miles of scenic rivers to explore. This area was established as a national park in 1941—the second-oldest national tourist attraction after Niagara Falls—and is a popular place for people from all over the world. Mammoth Cave was designated a World Heritage Site in 1981 and has become the core area of an International Biosphere Reserve because of its spectacular features, including 350-million-year-old rocks and animals that have adapted to life in the dark.

Visitors can choose from among several tours, ranging from an hour to more than six hours, which all begin at the visitors center. Some are geared toward children; others are more strenuous. One of the treks, the Grand Avenue Tour, allows guests to dine some 267 feet underground in the Snowball Dining Room; another showcases

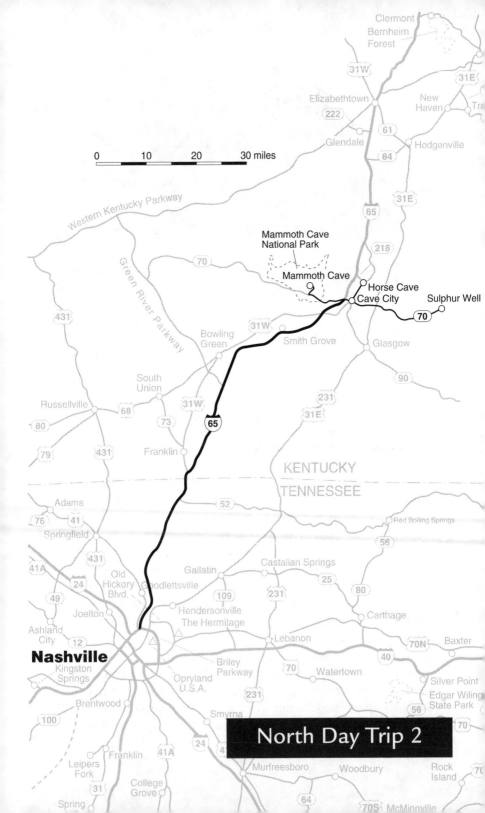

Clermont
Bernheim
Forest

31W
31E

Elizabethtown
222

New Haven
Tra

61
Glendale
84
Hodgenville

65
31E

218

Mammoth Cave
National Park

Western Kentucky Parkway

70

Mammoth Cave
Horse Cave
Cave City
Sulphur Well
70

431

Green River Parkway

Bowling Green
31W
Smith Grove
Glasgow

South Union
231
90

Russellville
68
31W
231
31E

80
73
65

79
431
Franklin

KENTUCKY

TENNESSEE

Adams
52
Red Boiling Springs

76
41
Springfield
56

41A
24
431
Gallatin
Castalian Springs
25

49
Old Hickory Blvd.
Goodlettsville
109
231
80
Carthage

Joelton
Hendersonville
The Hermitage
70N
Baxter

Ashland City
12
Lebanon
40

Nashville
Kingston Springs
Briley Parkway
70
Watertown
Silver Point

Opryland U.S.A.
Edgar Wiling
State Park

Brentwood
231
56
70

100
Smyrna

Franklin
41A
24
North Day Trip 2

Leipers Fork
Murfreesboro
Woodbury
Rock Island
70

Spring
College Grove
64
70S
McMinnville

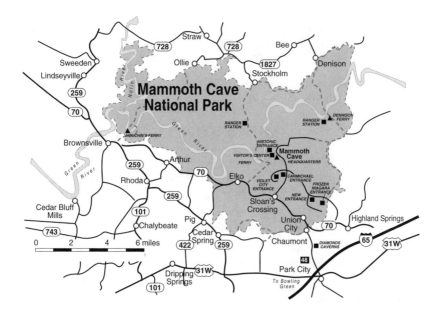

prehistoric artifacts, ruins of a saltpeter mining operation, and some of the largest rooms in the cave.

The best thing to do to familiarize yourself with the site is see the film when you arrive. Pick up a map and a park newspaper that details the ranger-led activities on the surface. Don't forget to wear sturdy walking shoes, and pack a light jacket, too. The temperature of the massive cavern hovers in the mid-fifties. Open daily except Christmas Day. Some tours are seasonal, and there are nightly programs during part of the year. Fee for adults; under six free. Tours for the disabled are offered. Tickets are available in advance for cave tours, (800) 967-2283. For park information, call (270) 758-2328, or see www.nps.gov/maca/home.htm or reservations.nps.gov. For accommodations within the park, call (270) 758-2225.

Miss Green River II. 511 Grinstead Mill Road. Take a one-hour ride on a 63-foot riverboat and admire the scenery and wildlife of Mammoth Cave National Park. The boat concession is authorized by the National Park Service. Open daily April through October. Call about special moonlight cruises on holiday weekends. Fee. (270) 758-2243.

CAVE CITY

From Mammoth Cave, head east on KY-70, crossing I-65. Cave City is situated 1 mile north on US-31W.

WHERE TO GO

Cave City Convention Center. 502 Mammoth Cave Street (KY-70). Pick up brochures for the attractions, hotels, and eating spots in Cave Country here. Open Monday through Saturday. (800) 346-8908 or (270) 773-3131; www.cavecity.com.

Crystal Onyx Cave and Campground. KY-90 east. This Kentucky cave features the typical stalactites, stalagmites, and other formations, but it also serves as a working archaeological site. Guided tours are offered daily. The campground is 300 feet above the valley and offers tent and RV camping. Open daily. Closed in January. (270) 773-2359; www.crystalonyxcave.com.

Guntown Mountain Amusement Park. KY-70 west at I-65. Not quite a mountain, but the chairlift takes guests up some 1,300 feet for a view of the Cave Country landscape. The Wild West town entertains with gunfights, rides, a haunted house, and the Onyx Cave tour. Open daily Memorial Day through Labor Day; weekends during May and from Labor Day through mid-October. Fee. (270) 773-3530; www.mammothcave.com/guntown.

Kentucky Action Park. KY-70 west (1½ miles off I-65). Here the whole family can enjoy go-carts, bumper boats, miniature golf, horseback riding, and a quarter-mile-long alpine slide and chairlift. Open daily Memorial Day through Labor Day; weekends Easter to Memorial Day and Labor Day through October. Fee. (270) 773-2636; www.mammothcave.com/kyaction.htm.

WHERE TO SHOP

There are numerous retail stores in the area that sell concrete statues, crafts, moccasins, and rocks. Shop around for the best prices.

Smith's Country Store. KY-70 west at I-65. It's hard to miss Smith's, which sits up on a hillside right off the interstate. The original country store dates back to 1906, but the newer location still draws people in for its great-tasting country hams and bacon, smoked sausage, and homemade jams, jellies, and relishes. Open daily. (270) 773-3530; www.mammothcave.com/guntown/smiths.

WHERE TO EAT

A slew of fast-food and chain restaurants are right off I-65 at the Cave City exit, or you can get a taste of Cave Country at one of the following.

Lighthouse Restaurant. KY-70 east, Sulphur Well. A twenty-minute drive east from the cave region lands you in the small town of Sulphur Well. "Kentucky's Original Country Ham Place" specializes in country ham dinners, served family-style with stewed potatoes, beans, slaw, tomatoes, fried apples, and biscuits and gravy. Fried chicken, catfish, sandwiches, and homemade pies round out the menu. Open for lunch and dinner Tuesday through Saturday, but breakfast served anytime. $-$$; credit cards not accepted. (270) 565-3095; www.sulpherwellky.com/lighthouse.

Mario's Italian Restaurant. 403 Mammoth Cave Road (on KY-70, between US-31W and I-65). Here proprietor Mario Rizzitiello serves up traditional Italian fare, with all food prepared to order. Lasagna, fettuccini Alfredo, Italian pastries, and cheesecake draw customers to this refurbished house, conveniently located between Cave City and Horse Cave. Open for dinner. Call ahead for hours. $$. (270) 773-5407.

Sahara Steak House. 413 Happy Valley Road. For more than twenty years this casual dining spot has specialized in steaks, seafood, and prime rib. Open for lunch and dinner daily. $$-$$$. (270) 773-3450.

WHERE TO STAY

There are several modern hotels just off the interstate, as well as campgrounds in the area. Mammoth Cave National Park also has a hotel, motor lodge, and cottages available.

Wigwam Village. US-31W, 601 North Dixie Highway. These fifteen concrete tepees built around a mini-park offer an unusual overnight experience. The wigwam design was patented in 1936, and there is only one other similar motel complex left in the country—in Holbrook, Arizona. Window air-conditioning units and cable TV have been added, but the tepees are still a throwback to a forgotten era of two-lane highways and tourist courts. The 52-foot-tall center wigwam houses the office and gift shop. Even if you're not spending the night, stop and browse through the wide array of gifts. You'll come out smiling. Closed December 1 through March 1. $–$$. (270) 773–3381; www.wigwamvillage.com.

HORSE CAVE

Horse Cave, the most northern of the three cities in the Mammoth Cave region, is partially situated over Hidden River Cave, whose underground river was once the source of the town's drinking water. Horse Cave is approximately 7 miles north of Cave City on I–65 and is a big tobacco-producing area.

WHERE TO GO

American Cave Museum and Hidden River Cave. 119 East Main Street. This museum, an environmental education center, presents tourists with exhibits detailing how caves are formed, plus a two-story replica of a cave chamber. Visitors also can walk outside to see the entrance to Hidden River Cave, and tours into the cave are available. Open daily year-round (call for winter hours). Fee. (270) 786–1466; www.cavern.org.

Kentucky Down Under/Kentucky Caverns. P.O. Box 189 (KY–218 and KY–335), 42749. Believe it or not, in the middle of South Central Kentucky you can see kangaroos, wallabies, tropical birds, and kookaburras. This seventy-five-acre wildlife refuge offers a petting area, a walk-in aviary where you can handle birds, and a souvenir and rock shop. A forty-five-minute tour of Kentucky Caverns—one of the area's easiest to navigate—is part of the ticket price. The animal park is open daily April through October; the cave is open daily year-round except Thanksgiving, Christmas, and New Year's Day. Fee. (800) 762–2869 or (270) 786–2634; www.kdu.com.

Kentucky Repertory Theatre at Horse Cave. 107 East Main Street. Although this small town is a most unlikely place for a nationally recognized repertory theater, it nonetheless offers one of a handful of rural professional theaters in the United States. Here guests can enjoy six productions in rotating repertory by playwrights such as Samuel Beckett, William Shakespeare, and Eugene O'Neill. The theater even invites Kentucky playwrights to showcase their work as part of its "Kentucky Voices"—the only program in the state for developing original Kentucky plays and playwrights. The auditorium seats almost 350 people, and the lobby serves as a gallery for rotating art exhibits. Open June through October, unless a Christmas play is scheduled for November/December. Fee. (800) 342-2177 or (270) 786-2177; www.horsecavetheatre.org.

WHERE TO SHOP

Caveland Shopping Center. Exit 58 off I-65. If you need a break from the underground world of caves, there's plenty of above-ground exploring to do at these factory outlet stores. Acme Boot, Casual Corner, Merry-Go-Round, Sander's Antiques, and Bugle Boy are just some of the retail shops located here. Open daily except Thanksgiving and Christmas. (270) 786-4446.

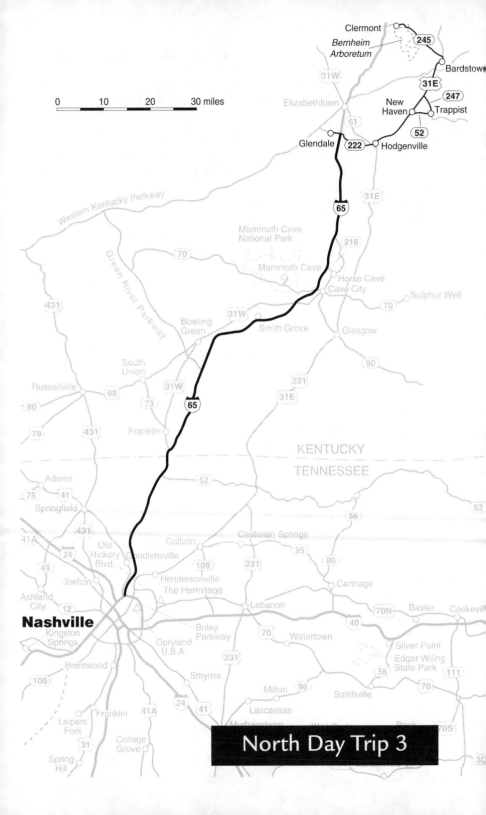

Clermont

Bernheim Arboretum

245

Bardstow

31W

31E

Elizabethtown

247

New Haven   Trappist

61

52

Glendale

222   Hodgenville

65   31E

Mammoth Cave
National Park

218

Mammoth Cave

Western Kentucky Parkway

Horse Cave
Cave City

70   Sulphur Well

431

Green River Parkway

31W

Bowling
Green   Smith Grove   Glasgow

90

South
Union

Russellville

68   31W

73   231

65   31E

80   431   Franklin

79

KENTUCKY

Adams   52   TENNESSEE   52

76   41

Springfield   56

431

Castalian Springs

41A   24   Old
Hickory
Blvd.

Gallatin

Goodlettsville   25   80

49

109   231   Carthage

Joelton   Hendersonville
The Hermitage

Ashland
City   12

Lebanon   70N   Baxter   Cookevil

Nashville

Kingston
Springs   Opryland
U.S.A.   Briley
Parkway   70   Watertown   40

Silver Point

Edgar Wiling
State Park   111

Brentwood   231   56   70

100   Smyrna

Franklin   41A   Milton   96   Smithville

Leipers
Fork   31   24   41   Lascassas   70S

College
Grove   Murfreesboro   30

Spring
Hill

North Day Trip 3

0   10   20   30 miles

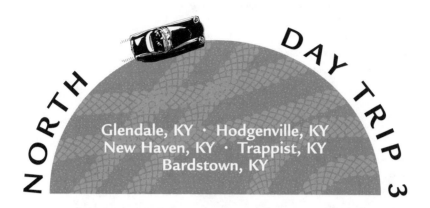

GLENDALE

A little less than two hours from Nashville on I-65 north, you will find the quaint community of Glendale, a National Historic District. Take exit 86 off I-65, and then travel 2 miles west on KY-222 into town. Antiques shops, restaurants, and Kentucky craft outlets line the street, which is located near the Nashville/Louisville railroad tracks. Glendale was a bustling passenger stop in the early 1900s, and the charm of the town is still intact. The Glendale Crossing Festival is held every October and features arts and crafts, antique machinery demonstrations, and music (see "Festivals and Celebrations"). This area of Kentucky is on eastern time.

WHERE TO SHOP

Glendale's Main Street is an antiques shopper's haven. There are a number of antiques malls filled with linens and glassware, as well as places that specialize in Blue Ridge pottery, antique wicker, and Victorian furniture. Call the Glendale Merchants Association, (270) 737-6444, for a complete listing of stores, or visit www .historicglendale.com/.

WHERE TO EAT

The Depot Restaurant. Main Street and Railroad Avenue. The Depot specializes in steaks, prime rib, catfish, and flowerpot bread (baked in a clay pot). Choices vary, and homemade desserts top off the meal. The waiting area displays a fun collection of Mickey Mouse memorabilia and toy trains. Open daily for lunch and dinner. $–$$. (270) 369–6000.

The Whistle Stop. 216 East Main Street. This cozy restaurant, which opened in 1975, is situated right next to the railroad tracks. A wide array of entrees is served up here, from country ham to rainbow trout. Homemade soups and yeast breads, plus freshly made desserts, are also always on tap. Open Tuesday through Saturday for lunch and dinner. Prepare to wait on weekends for a table, but go ahead and browse Main Street—the restaurant will page you when your table is ready. $–$$. (270) 369–8586.

WHERE TO STAY

Petticoat Junction Bed and Breakfast. 223 High Street. A splendid place to bed down after a day of antiquing is the homey Petticoat Junction, located just off Main Street. The six rooms in this 1870s farmhouse are nicely appointed, and beautiful herb and perennial gardens also beckon visitors. A full country breakfast is included, as well as cookies and coffee in the evening. An antiques store, The Sisters Shop, is located next door. Petticoat Junction is convenient for exploring nearby Hodgenville, too. $$. (270) 369–8604 or (800) 308–0364.

HODGENVILLE

A few miles east of Glendale will bring you to Hodgenville, where Abraham Lincoln was born. The small town takes great pride in its famous offspring, and anything and everything is named after him—from Lincoln National Bank to the Lincoln Memorial Motel. The town square—called Lincoln Square—sports a bronze statue of the former president that was commissioned by Congress and erected in 1909. The Lincoln Days Celebration, held in October, commemorates his birth with a parade, pioneer games, craft demonstrations, and a Lincoln look-alike contest (see "Festivals and Celebrations").

WHERE TO GO

LaRue County Chamber of Commerce. 58 Lincoln Square. The chamber is conveniently located in Hodgenville's town square. Stop by for brochures and information. The Lincoln Museum, a newly renovated space with many artifacts, is right next door. Call (270) 358-3163 for the Museum. Open Monday through Friday. (270) 358-3411; www.laruecountychamber.org.

    Abraham Lincoln Birthplace National Historic Site. US-31E and KY-61 (3 miles south of Hodgenville). It was on this farm called Sinking Spring that the sixteenth president of the United States was born in 1809. The 116-acre site, with its marble and granite memorial, is one of the most visited shrines in the country.

    Climb the fifty-six steps (one for each year of Lincoln's life) to see the log cabin traditionally thought of as Lincoln's birthplace, and visit Sinking Spring, where the Lincolns drew their water. The visitor center houses exhibits and an audiovisual program on the president's childhood. Picnic facilities and hiking trails are also located here, and special events occur year-round. Open daily except Thanksgiving and Christmas. Wheelchair accessible. Free. (270) 358-3137; www.nps.gov/abli/linchomj.htm.

    Abraham Lincoln's Boyhood Home. US-31E north (7 miles north of town). Knob Creek Farm is where Lincoln spent five years as a young boy, and he once wrote that his earliest memories of Kentucky were "of the Knob Creek place." Here visitors can see a reproduction of the cabin similar to the one in which Lincoln lived until he was almost eight years old. There is also a large souvenir shop filled with Lincoln memorabilia and artifacts. Knob Creek Farm is on the National Register of Historic Places and has been part of the National Park Service since 2002. Guided tours are available, and you can spread a picnic lunch under a shaded pavilion. Open daily April through October. Fee. (270) 549-3741.

    Lincoln Jamboree. 2579 Lincoln Farm Road (US-31E). Country music is the featured attraction at the Jamboree, which has been drawing visitors since 1954. Tickets are sold in advance for a show every Saturday night year-round. Fee. (270) 358-3545.

WHERE TO EAT

Joel Ray's Family Restaurant. 2579 Lincoln Farm Road (next door to the Lincoln Jamboree). Five years after starting the Jamboree, the owner opened this cafeteria-style restaurant next door. "Country cooked" meats and vegetables are offered in addition to breakfast fare. Open daily except Monday for all three meals. $; credit cards not accepted. (270) 358-3545.

NEW HAVEN

A few miles north of Knob Creek on US–31E is the small town of New Haven, Kentucky.

WHERE TO GO

Kentucky Railway Museum. US–31E. Ride the rails on the Kentucky Railway Museum train between New Haven and neighboring Boston, Kentucky. The 22-mile round-trip ride carries you through scenic farmland and a few small communities in the Rolling Fork River Valley. One steam locomotive dates from 1905, and there are other vintage coaches and memorabilia at the depot in the museum store. Trains run on Saturday, Sunday, and major holidays from May through mid-December. From June through August, the train ride is also offered Tuesday through Friday. Closed Sunday and Monday in January and February. Special events throughout the year. Fee. (800) 272-0152 or (502) 549-5470; www.kyrail.org.

WHERE TO STAY AND EAT

The Sherwood Inn. 138 South Main Street. This historic inn, located next to the Kentucky Railway Museum, has fed and lodged numerous travelers since it opened in 1875, and it has been owned by descendants of the same family since it began operating. The inn, which is situated on the railroad line, offers a complete dinner menu, with chicken, beef, pork, fish, and pasta entrees that are accompanied by salad and homemade bread. The restaurant also hosts banquets and parties and serves lunch and dinner on the Kentucky Railway Museum train by reservation. Five upstairs guest rooms furnished in

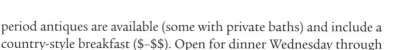

period antiques are available (some with private baths) and include a country-style breakfast ($-$$). Open for dinner Wednesday through Saturday. $$. (502) 549–3386; www.thesherwoodinn.net.

TRAPPIST

WHERE TO GO

Abbey of Gethsemani. 3642 Monks Road. Continue on US–31E north for a few miles until you reach KY–247. Head east for about 4 miles until you see the Abbey of Gethsemani nestled on a hillside. Noted for "prayer, labor, and silence," here dwells the largest and oldest monastery of Cistercian monks in the United States, with approximately seventy monks in residence now (average age about sixty). Gethsemani also was the home of well-known author Thomas Merton until his death in 1968. The striking monastery, founded in 1848, is known worldwide for its bourbon-laced fruitcakes, Port Salut cheeses, and bourbon fudge, all of which are produced on the premises. The public is invited to attend prayer services, held several times throughout the day, and take home a mail-order catalog of the monastery's products. The abbey offers facilities for retreats, too, on its 2,400 acres. Open year-round. Free. (502) 549–3117; www.monks.org. Retreat reservations can be made by calling (502) 549–4133.

BARDSTOWN

Get back on US–31E and travel north for about 10 miles to reach Bardstown, known as the "Bourbon Capital of the World." The surrounding area once had twenty-two operating distilleries, and four still remain open. Bardstown is situated in one of the few "wet" counties in the Commonwealth, meaning you can buy and sell whiskey legally. The attractive town, with its stately homes and manicured lawns, is also recognized for "My Old Kentucky Home," the song composer Stephen Foster wrote after visiting Federal Hill Manor there. The community of 10,374 residents, formerly known as Salem, also boasts the oldest western stagecoach stop in America. Tourism is Bardstown's major industry. Bardstown is home to several festivals, including My Old Kentucky Home Festival of Quilts in March, the Kentucky Bourbon Festival in September, and the Kentucky Music Weekend in July (see "Festivals and Celebrations").

WHERE TO GO

Bardstown Visitors' Information Center. 107 East Stephen Foster Avenue. This center is well equipped to provide information to visitors, offering maps, brochures, and a video on Bardstown's attractions. The town's historic walking tour and the free Tourmobile, which operates from June until Labor Day, start here. The Tourmobile drives by local attractions over the course of fifty minutes, making one stop at Heaven Hill Distilleries. Open daily, May through September. (800) 638–4877 or (502) 348–4877; www.visit bardstown.com/tourism.

Bernheim Arboretum and Research Center. KY–245 (15 miles west of Bardstown), Clermont. If you enjoy the beauty of the woods, then take the short drive from Bardstown to the Bernheim Arboretum, celebrating its seventy-fifth anniversary in 2004. A small section of this 14,000-acre wildlife sanctuary has been developed with an arboretum. (A new visitor center opened in late 2004.) There are 35 miles of self-guided nature trails through the woods, plus exhibits detailing native animals and birds. Open year-round, but closed Christmas Day and New Year's Day. Free on weekdays; vehicle fee on weekends. (502) 955–8512; www.bernheim.org.

Distillery Tours. Two distilleries in the Bardstown area are open for free tours—Heaven Hill (502–348–3921) and Maker's Mark (270–865–2099). Jim Beam Distillery shows a video of the production process, and tourists can see exhibits about whiskey making and visit the gift shop. (502) 543–9877. Most tours are conducted Monday through Saturday, but call ahead for times.

Heaven Hill Distilleries. KY–49 (1 mile south of Bardstown). This is the largest family-owned distillery in the country and the closest to Bardstown. Evan Williams and Elijah Craig bourbon whiskeys (distilled from a corn-bread mash) are made here and shipped all over the world. While the law prohibits giving away free tastes, the smell is satisfying enough. Two tours are offered Monday through Friday. Group tours by reservation. Free. (502) 348-3921; www.heaven-hill.com.

My Old Kentucky Home State Park. US-150 east. This is the location of the three-story brick mansion, formerly known as Federal Hill, that was immortalized in Stephen Foster's ballad. The home is now the focal point of the park, which was established in 1922. The area offers an eighteen-hole golf course, picnic grounds, camping facilities, and a visitor center with an extensive gift shop. Tours by guides in antebellum costumes show off the 1818 home's furnishings, gardens, carriage house, and smokehouse. Christmas Candlelight Tours are held Friday, Saturday, and Sunday for the three weeks following Thanksgiving. Open daily year-round except Thanksgiving Day, Christmas week, and New Year's Eve and Day. Fee. (800) 323-7803 or (502) 348-3502; www.state.ky.us/agencies/parks/ky home.htm.

Oscar Getz Museum of Whiskey History. 114 North Fifth Street (behind St. Joseph Proto-Cathedral). Spalding Hall has had numerous functions over the years, from a college and seminary to a hospital for the armies during the Civil War. It now houses the Oscar Getz Museum of Whiskey History, Bardstown Historical Museum, and a restaurant. The Oscar Getz Museum contains a fifty-year collection of various documents and artifacts on the whiskey industry. Copper distilling vessels and some 200 bottles and jugs are on display as well as white oak barrels used in the operation. The Historical Museum documents Bardstown's history with Indian relics, Stephen Foster memorabilia, Civil War artifacts, and Abraham Lincoln materials. Both museums open daily May through October; closed Monday November through April. Free. Small donation requested. (502) 348-2999.

Stephen Foster—The Musical. US-150 east (My Old Kentucky Home State Park Amphitheater). Held on the grounds of the former plantation that inspired the song "My Old Kentucky Home," this outdoor production has been entertaining audiences since 1959. More than 300 costumes and fifty Foster songs combine to make an enjoyable evening of outdoor theater, especially since more than $1 million was poured into renovations in 1997. It's a lovely way to end a day, watching the sun set as you listen to "Jeannie with the Light Brown Hair" and "Camptown Races." Another production, *Showboat,* is also offered, as are special Halloween performances in October.

Call ahead for a schedule and hours. Open early June through the end of August, with performances nightly except Monday. A Saturday matinee is held at the indoor theater. Fee. (800) 626–1563 or (502) 348–5971; www.stephenfoster.com.

St. Joseph Proto-Cathedral. 310 West Stephen Foster Avenue. This was the first Catholic cathedral west of the Allegheny Mountains and is listed by the Library of Congress as a National Landmark. The attractive, white-columned church contains a valuable collection of seventeenth-century European paintings. Guided tours offered daily from early spring through October 31. Small donation requested. (502) 348–3126.

Wickland. US–62 (1 mile east of Court Square). This 180-year-old mansion, said to be one of the finest examples of Georgian architecture in the country, was the home of three governors. A guided tour explains the home's history and beautiful antique furnishings. Open by appointment. Fee. (502) 348–5428.

WHERE TO EAT

Dagwood's. 204 North Third Street. The "Elijah Craig," a New York strip steak marinated in twelve-year-old Elijah Craig bourbon, is the specialty here and a meal for hearty appetites. Sample the terrific three-cheese potatoes, too, served up with a soup and salad bar that is fresh and tasty. Open for lunch and dinner Monday through Saturday. $–$$. (502) 348–4029.

Kreso's Restaurant. 218 North Third Street. Stop in Kreso's for one of the tasty sandwiches, or opt for one of the entrees, especially those derived from Eastern European recipes. Diners will find beef goulash, shish kebab, and Wiener schnitzel, as well as American mainstays such as steak, salmon, and grilled chicken. The eatery also offers unusual beers and a selection of gourmet coffee drinks as well as dessert. Music is often scheduled on weekends. Open Monday through Saturday for lunch and dinner. $–$$. (502) 348–9594.

Kurtz Restaurant. 418 East Stephen Foster Avenue. Open since 1937, it's a convenient spot to grab some dinner before heading to "Stephen Foster—The Musical" (it's right across the street from My Old Kentucky Home State Park). Turkey breast, skillet-fried chicken, and tender roast beef are served family-style with bowls of green beans, spiced beets, and hot bread. Open daily for lunch and dinner. $–$$. (502) 348-8964.

My Old Kentucky Dinner Train. 602 North Third Street. Several 1940s dining cars have been restored and now serve as a rolling restaurant. Travel from Bardstown to Limestone Springs through the Bernheim Arboretum while dining on a tasty three-course meal for lunch or five courses for dinner. Two-hour lunch and dinner excursions by reservation. Open Tuesday through Saturday; weekends during the winter. Fee. (502) 348-7500; www.kydinnertrain.com.

The Old Talbott Tavern. 107 West Stephen Foster Avenue. Known as the oldest western stagecoach stop in America, the Talbott has been serving guests almost continually since 1779 (a devastating fire in 1998 caused the inn and restaurant to close for several months). Present-day guests dine in the same rooms as did Daniel Boone, Abraham Lincoln, Gen. George Rogers Clark, and John J. Audubon. The bullet holes in the murals are said to have come from Jesse James's gun. With more than two centuries of feeding travelers behind it, Talbott Tavern draws a large crowd for its fried chicken, country ham, pot roast, and homemade cobblers. The Bourbon Bar offers snacks, refreshments, and live entertainment on weekends. Five guest rooms—named after both the famous and infamous—are decorated in period antiques and come with modern amenities. A full breakfast greets guests on weekends; with a continental breakfast on weekdays. The gift shop carries a wide array of souvenirs and Kentucky cookbooks, and Talbott Tavern also caters and hosts weddings. Open daily for lunch and dinner. $$–$$$. (800) 4TAVERN or (502) 348-3494; www.talbotts.com.

WHERE TO STAY

There are more than a dozen bed-and-breakfasts in the Bardstown area as well as several motels. Call the visitor center (800-638-4877) for a complete listing.

A RoseMark Haven Bed and Breakfast. 714 North Third Street. A short distance from downtown, this 1830 antebellum mansion features seven spacious rooms with fine antiques, a lovely entry foyer, and covered porches in the front and back. A gourmet breakfast is included in the price. $$–$$$. (502) 348-8218 or (888) 420-9703; www.arosemarkhaven.com.

Jailer's Inn Bed and Breakfast. 111 West Stephen Foster Avenue. For a unique lodging experience, spend the night in Bardstown's old jail, which housed prisoners up until 1987. The five guest rooms are well decorated and quite large, and a full breakfast is served in the outdoor courtyard when weather permits. The sixth guest room still resembles a cell, outfitted with two of the original bunk beds. Out back, you can see where the hangings took place and tour the "dungeon," which has remained virtually untouched for more than 170 years. Jailer's Inn is convenient to the city's many attractions, and tours of the jail are conducted daily for a modest fee. $$. (502) 348-5551; www.jailersinn.com.

Victorian Lights Bed and Breakfast. 112 South Third Street. Right off the Courthouse Square is this pretty Victorian home, built in the Queen Anne architectural style. Three guest rooms with private baths are available (one has a sitting room and whirlpool), and your stay includes a full breakfast served in the formal dining room. This bed-and-breakfast is situated in a quiet residential area and has smoke-free rooms. $$. (502) 348-8087.

OPRYLAND

The Opryland Area is located 9 miles northeast of Nashville. Take exit 11 off Briley Parkway between I-40 and I-65 to get to the Opry Plaza and the Grand Ole Opry building; take exit 12 to get to the hotel.

Many people associate the name Opryland with the theme park, which closed in 1998. However, the area now includes a huge complex of entertainment and lodging facilities owned by Gaylord Entertainment. Among the company's attractions (some are located in downtown Nashville), the Grand Ole Opry, the Gaylord Opryland Resort and Convention Center, the Ryman Auditorium, Wildhorse Saloon, Grand Ole Opry Tours, Springhouse Golf Club, and the vast Opry Mills. Visit www.gaylordhotels.com/gaylordopryland.

WHERE TO GO

General Jackson **Showboat.** Opryland's showboat entertains guests with year-round sightseeing, dining, and entertainment cruises. Day and evening excursions on the 300-foot-long paddle wheeler meander up and down the Cumberland River. Meal service is optional on the day cruises; the dinner trip includes a seated banquet in the price and a stage production. Call for times and tickets. Fee. (615) 889-6611.

The Grand Ole Opry. If you're a country music fan or just want to experience the longest-running radio show in the world, don't miss The Grand Ole Opry. The Opry has been entertaining guests

29

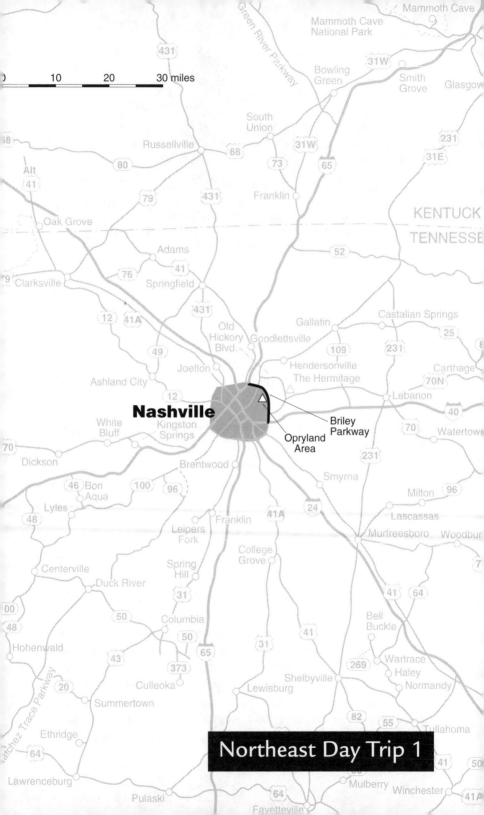

Northeast Day Trip 1

with both up-and-comers and Hall-of-Famers since it began in 1925, and the show has never missed a broadcast. Each performance features about twenty-five country music acts singing country, bluegrass, gospel, Cajun, and Western swing. The artist line-up is scheduled each week, so the show is always one-of-a-kind. Open Friday and Saturday nights year-round.

Opry Mills. Opry Mills, which opened in 2000, combines more than 225 retail shops, restaurants, and entertainment venues. Bass Pro Shops Outdoor World, a 135,000-square-foot store, is one of its key anchors. Nike Factory Store, Old Navy, Rainforest Cafe, Alabama Grill, and an eighteen-screen Regal Cinemas and IMAX 3-D Theater are located in the 1.2-million-square-foot complex. An entertainment corridor connects the General Jackson, Grand Ole Opry, and other parts of the Gaylord-owned property. Opry Mills replaces the Opryland theme park, which closed in 1998 after drawing tourists for twenty-six years.

The Opry Plaza. The Plaza is home to the Grand Ole Opry Museum, which showcases the history of the famous radio show with memorabilia from Opry folks such as Lorrie Morgan, Marty Stuart, Reba McEntire, Roy Acuff, and Minnie Pearl. Gaze at a re-creation of Patsy Cline's living room or Marty Robbins's "garage." Country stars from Little Jimmy Dickens to Elvis are represented by guitars, costumes, photographs, song drafts, fiddles, and so on. Starwalk, just outside the museum, is where Nashville's Grammy Award-winners have left their hand- and footprints. The Plaza area is nicely planted, and benches are scattered about if you need a break. www.opry.com.

WHERE TO STAY AND EAT

Gaylord Opryland Resort and Convention Center. This massive hotel, which is the largest combined hotel and convention center under one roof anywhere, is an indoor walker's dream. You can get lost in the maze of hallways or eight acres of indoor gardens. The glass-topped conservatory is home to a jungle of tropical plants and flowers, and Cascades is a water-themed area with waterfalls and a 12,500-square-foot lake. The hotel has twenty-five restaurants and lounges, an eighteen-hole championship golf course, thirty retail shops, ballrooms, two swimming pools, and a fitness center. The number of guest rooms is almost 3,000, with a four-

and-a-half-acre "interiorscape" that includes a flowing river, twenty-five-passenger flatboats, Southern-style shops, and street vendors. Banquet rooms in The Delta overlook an 85-foot fountain, 110-foot-wide waterfall, a 400-seat restaurant called Old Hickory Steakhouse, and an intimate garden for private receptions. Garden terrace rooms overlook some of the indoor plantings, and there are more than 200 suites at the hotel. There is always some convention or other happening at Opryland, drawing visitors from around the world. Vacation packages are offered. $$$. (615) 889–1000; www.oprylandhotels.com.

HENDERSONVILLE

Say "Hendersonville," and most folks immediately think of two things: Old Hickory Lake and the spectacular homes of country music stars that dot the lake area. Located only 23 miles northeast of downtown Nashville, this fast-growing community boasts 26 miles of Old Hickory Lake shoreline and is a short drive out Gallatin Road or US–31E.

WHERE TO GO

Historic Rock Castle. 139 Rock Castle Lane. Rock Castle, located 2 miles south of Gallatin Road (US–31E), is on the National Register of Historic Places. General Daniel Smith, one of Tennessee's early statesmen and a well-known surveyor credited with producing the first map of Tennessee, made Rock Castle his home. Built of limestone quarried nearby, the home is furnished in late-eighteenth-century style and contains many original pieces, including the family Bible, private letters, and more than 200 of Smith's books. Open daily March through December. Fee. (615) 824–0502; www.historic rockcastle.cjb.net.

Trinity Music City USA. 1 Music Village Boulevard. Go out US–31E or take exit 95 off I–65. The former home and grounds of country music star Conway Twitty are now part of the worldwide religious television network, Trinity Broadcasting. The complex has a theater where visitors can see free live television tapings and musical entertainment, as well as a virtual reality theater showing a film about

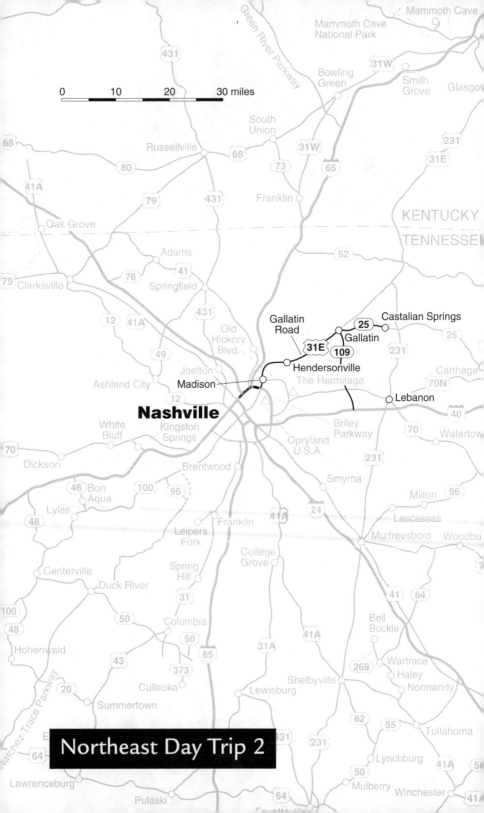

Northeast Day Trip 2

the life of Christ. The gardens and mansion are also open for touring, and a gift shop and restaurant are located on the premises. The place comes alive late November through December with more than one million lights and special performances (see "Festivals and Celebrations"). Open daily. Free. Call (615) 826–9191 for recorded information; for other assistance, call (615) 822–8333 or visit www.tbn.org.

WHERE TO EAT

Center Point Barbecue. 1212 West Main Street. Some people claim this small barbecue joint is one of the best, serving up pork (order it on corn bread), chicken, and hickory-smoked baby back ribs. The eatery has been a mainstay in Hendersonville since 1965 and is open for breakfast, lunch, and dinner every day, but it closes at 5:00 P.M. on Sunday. $-$$; credit cards not accepted. (615) 824–9330.

The Shack. 2420 Gallatin Road North, Madison. The Shack may as well have a Hendersonville address because it's only a couple of miles south of downtown. This casual eatery has been a mainstay since 1965 and is known for its seafood, steaks, and prime rib, as well as for the roasted peanut shells that cover the floor. Try the charbroiled shrimp, and while you're waiting, munch on some of the addictive roasted nuts. Open daily for dinner, and for lunch and dinner on Sunday. $$. (615) 859–9777.

GALLATIN AND CASTALIAN SPRINGS

From Hendersonville, continue on US–31E for about ten minutes until you reach Gallatin. If you're enamored with the charm of historic homes, then the Gallatin area is the place to visit. A self-guided tour—The Path of the Longhunters—takes travelers to some of the oldest sites in Middle Tennessee. Stop by the Sumner County Tourism office for a brochure at 118 West Main Street. (615) 230–8474; www.sumnercountytourism.com.

WHERE TO GO

Cragfont. TN–25, Castalian Springs. Six miles east of Gallatin on TN–25, Cragfont was the home of General James Winchester, who served in both the Revolutionary War and the War of 1812. The three-story Federal-style building and an adjoining garden have been restored, and a visit takes in interesting features such as stenciling on the parlor walls and original woodwork and flooring. Open Tuesday through Sunday, April 15 through October 31; other times by appointment. Fee. (615) 452-7070; www.srlab.net/cragfont.

Trousdale Place. 183 West Main Street, Gallatin. Just two city blocks from the public square, this two-story brick house was former Tennessee governor William Trousdale's home, built in 1813. The attractive residence gives visitors a look at period furnishings and a military history library. The Sumner County Museum (615-451-3738) is located in the back of Trousdale Place and documents life in the county from the days of the Indians to the present. The three-story carriage house exhibits more than 250,000 artifacts. Both Trousdale Place and the museum are open by appointment. The home and grounds are used for teas, receptions, meetings, and weddings. Fee. (615) 452-5648; www.trousdaleplace.com.

Wynnewood. 210 Old Highway 25, Castalian Springs. Two miles farther east of Gallatin just off TN-25, this log structure, built in 1828 by Colonel A. R. Wynne, served as a stagecoach inn and mineral springs resort. At 142 feet long, Wynnewood is probably the largest log building ever constructed in Tennessee and contains early American furniture. Open daily April through October. Closed Sunday November through March. Also open by appointment. Fee. (615) 452-5463.

WHERE TO EAT

Cherokee Steak House. 450 Cherokee Dock Road (3½ miles south of Gallatin on TN-109), Lebanon. Since 1958 this dining spot has been serving up steaks, prime rib, and baby back ribs carved on the premises in Cherokee's own butcher shop. You can watch the boats go by on Old Hickory Lake as you savor catfish, country ham, chicken, and seafood. Open for dinner Tuesday through Sunday. $$. (615) 452-1515.

WHERE TO STAY

The Hancock House. 2144 Nashville Pike, Gallatin. Hancock House is conveniently situated on US-31E between Hendersonville and Gallatin. Four bedrooms await guests in this stately log inn, all with private baths and fireplaces. A two-story cabin across the lawn from the main house has a den with fireplace, kitchen, and whirlpool. In its former life, Hancock House was a pre-1878 stagecoach inn and tollgate house known as Avondale Station. A full country-style breakfast is served. The hosts also prepare a moderately priced breakfast, brunch, lunch, and dinner for inn guests and others with advance reservations. Plus, Hancock House is available for weddings, meetings, and parties. $$-$$$. (615) 452-8431; www.bbonline.com/tn/hancock.

Maple Shade Bed and Breakfast. 1755 Highway 31 East, Gallatin. This historic nineteenth-century house has three large guest rooms and an enclosed sleeping porch room. There's also a boxwood garden that's available for weddings and other special events. (615) 452-8282.

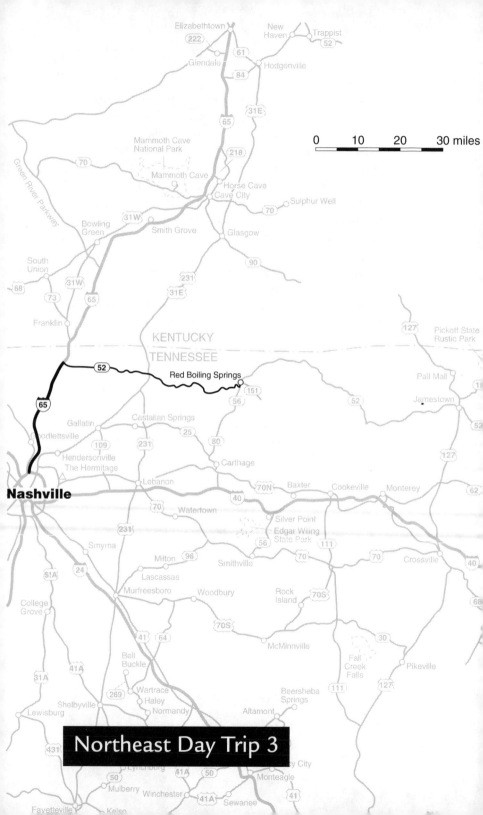

Northeast Day Trip 3

RED BOILING SPRINGS

From Nashville, it's a scenic ninety-minute drive to the small town of Red Boiling Springs. Take I-65 north, then head east on TN-52. A visit here is most definitely a step back in time. Little has changed in this small town except maybe the pace has slowed a bit. This tiny hamlet of little more than 1,000 residents was a popular resort community in the early 1900s. In those days, mineral waters said to have remarkable curative powers beckoned visitors from all over the world. "Red," "black," "white," "freestone," and "double and twist" were the names given to the sulphur-based waters.

Not only did travelers come to drink and bathe in the healing waters, but they stayed on to enjoy leisurely pastimes such as croquet, tennis, and dancing under the stars. From one hotel in 1860, the town grew to more than eight lodging spots and more than a dozen boarding houses. While that era has long passed, three hotels remain and so do the intriguing waters. Various working pumps still allow visitors to try a drink of red or black water. A Folk Medicine Festival (see "Festivals and Celebrations") held each July focuses on the history and practice of folk medicine and other aspects of back-to-basics living.

The Salt Lick Creek winds its way through this small Middle Tennessee town, and two picturesque covered bridges downtown give tourists reason to slow down to the pace of country life. There is not much to do in Red Boiling Springs except kick back and relax, eat some country cooking, and spend some quiet time reading in one of the hotels' many rocking chairs.

WHERE TO GO

Red Boiling Springs City Hall. 166 Dale Street. Stop by City Hall to pick up information about the history of the resort community and other helpful brochures. Open Monday through Friday. (615) 699–2011; www.redboilingspringstn.com.

WHERE TO SHOP

Check the local hotels for gift and antiques shops. Many, including Armour's Red Boiling Springs Hotel and The Thomas House, have shops as part of the hotel.

WHERE TO STAY AND EAT

Armour's Red Boiling Springs Hotel. 321 East Main Street (TN–151). This cozy hotel, built in 1924, is home to Tennessee's only operating mineral bathhouse. For a fee, you can experience both a soothing bath in the waters that made this town famous and a rubdown by one of the licensed massage therapists. All twenty-six rooms have private baths. Two hearty country meals are included in the room rate (reservations are necessary for meals). Even if you're not a guest at Armour's, you can still enjoy breakfast, lunch, or dinner with advance notice. $–$$. (615) 699–2180; www.armours hotel.com.

   The Donoho Hotel. 500 East Main Street. This two-story hotel has thirty-four guest rooms, all with private baths and no phones. Built in 1914, The Donoho sports a long white-columned porch that entices visitors to while away the afternoon in old-fashioned rocking chairs. An extensive renovation was finished in 2002. A dinner bell still rings to indicate it's time for one of the plentiful family-style meals. Country ham, fried chicken, biscuits, homemade jellies, and country-style vegetables arrive on large platters refilled when empty. Two meals are included in the room rate, and the dining room is open to other visitors with prior reservations. The Family Entertainment Theater features country music on Saturday night. $–$$. (615) 699–3141 or (800) 799–1705; www.thedonohohotel.com.

The Thomas House. 520 East Main Street. Some may recall this place when it was known as the Cloyd Hotel, named for the family that opened the hotel in 1890. The fifty-four-room structure was built from bricks that were molded and fired on the premises. Remodeled in 1993 and again in 2002 after a devastating fire, the lobby is a showplace for European antiques, sculptures, and crystal chandeliers. A hand-carved English oak mantel from the old Maxwell House Hotel is a focal point in the "gathering room." The large hotel has twenty-eight guest rooms, all with private baths. Amenities include a swimming pool, library, and several rooms full of memorabilia from the era. Like the other hotels here, two full meals, including a Sunday brunch buffet, are included in the room price, and they are offered (with advance reservations) to visitors who are not overnight guests at The Thomas House. The vast manicured lawn provides a place to stroll or relax with a book. Live music most weekends. $-$$. (615) 699-3006; www.thomashousehotel.com.

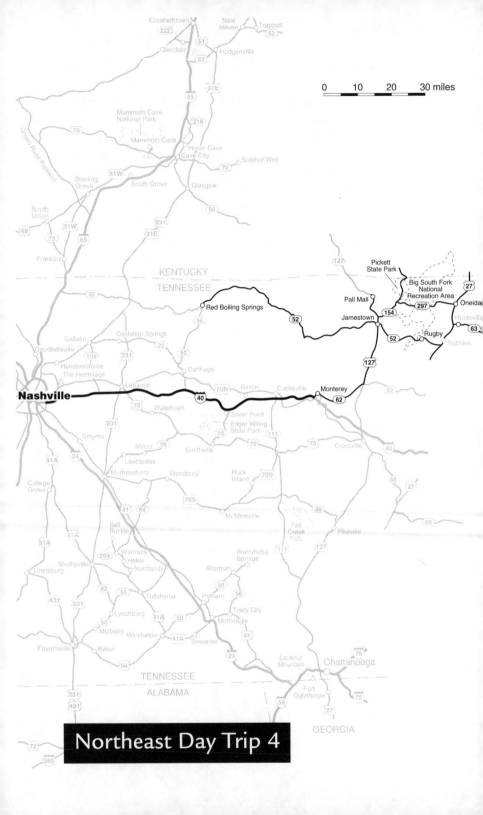

Northeast Day Trip 4

Jamestown, TN
Rugby, TN

JAMESTOWN

You could continue east on TN-52 from Red Boiling Springs all the way to Jamestown, but be forewarned—the pace is slow-going due to the winding roads through the hills of the Cumberland Plateau. The area is a beautiful place to enjoy the outdoors, with places to visit such as Big South Fork National River and Recreation Area, Pickett State Park, and nearby Dale Hollow Lake, which is a paradise for fishing, boating, and water sports. If you're a bargain-hunter, don't miss the annual 450 Mile Highway 127 Corridor Sale, the "World's Largest Outdoor Sale" each August (see "Festivals and Celebrations").

From Nashville, the best way to go is east on I-40 until you reach Monterey (exit 300). Continue east on TN-62 until you get to the US-127 junction, then head north on US-127 for about 15 miles until reaching Jamestown. Both Jamestown and Rugby are on eastern time.

WHERE TO GO

Highland Manor Winery. 2965 South York Highway. Situated 3 miles south of Jamestown, Highland Manor has the distinction of being the oldest licensed winery in Tennessee. Its white wines have won accolades in this country and abroad. Tours of the Tudor-style winery are offered, and picnicking is allowed on the landscaped grounds. Open daily year-round, except some Sundays in the winter months and on holidays. Free. (931) 879-9519; www.dalehollow.org/wines.

Big South Fork National River and Recreation Area. Route 3, P.O. Box 401, Oneida, TN 37841. From Jamestown, it's about 25 miles north on TN–154 (connecting with TN–297 east) to the visitor center at Big South Fork. This rugged region of the Cumberland Plateau offers boundless activities for the outdoor enthusiast. White-water canoeing, rafting, kayaking, mountain biking, hiking, hunting, fishing, and camping are great ways to enjoy the 105,000 acres of Big South Fork, which the National Park Service took over in 1974. For horseback riders, there are more than 130 miles of horse trails to blaze here, either on short rides or a three-day adventure (contact Bandy Creek Stables, 1845 Old Sunbright Road, Jamestown, TN 38556; 931–879–4013). Plus, if you're into primitive lodging accessible only by trail, you can drop your saddlebags at the Charit Creek Lodge, which is open year-round (see "Where to Stay"). For more information about Big South Fork, call (931) 879–3625, or visit www.bigsouthforkpark.com.

Pickett State Rustic Park and Forest. 4605 Pickett Park Highway (12 miles north of Jamestown). On the western border of Big South Fork is one of Tennessee's prettiest state parks. Its 12,000 acres are marked by interesting rock formations, natural bridges, and an abundance of wildflowers in the spring. There are nature trails, fishing, boating, tennis courts, cottages (including some rustic stone ones), and campgrounds, plus a beach for swimming during the summer. Naturalist programs are offered in the summer months. Free. (931) 879–5821; www.state.tn.us/environment/parks/parks/pickett.

Sgt. Alvin York's Gristmill and Park. US–127 north (7 miles north of Jamestown), Pall Mall. Sergeant York, legendary for his courageous action during World War I, was born and raised in the plateau region of Tennessee. The gristmill he operated is now a State Historic Area on the scenic Wolf River. Peek inside at some of the equipment used to grind grain. Swings, slides, and picnic tables make this a pleasant stopover for families. Open daily. Free. (931) 879–4026.

WHERE TO EAT

Bacara's. Wheeler Lane (off TN–297). Bacara's is a nice place to grab some grub after a day of hiking. The restaurant is housed in a 75-year-old schoolhouse and offers a continental dinner (the chef is originally from Germany), with steaks, homegrown vegetables, homemade soups, and fresh-baked bread. Open Wednesday through Friday for dinner; Saturday for lunch and dinner. Reservations are required. $$; credit cards not accepted. (931) 879-7121.

WHERE TO STAY

Charit Creek Lodge. Big South Fork National River and Recreation Area. For hearty souls who relish primitive accommodations accessible only by horse or hiking trail, this lodge offers a bona fide night in the wilderness and two substantial mountain meals cooked on propane and served in a cozy, paneled dining hall. Wood-burning stoves, kerosene lanterns, and bunk beds greet visitors, who either hike in or ride horses to the lodge, deep in the heart of Big South Fork. This is a place where the moon and stars take on added brightness on a clear night. The detached restrooms have running water, and the showers are heated by propane. Two separate cabins also accommodate guests and can be reserved by a whole party. Open year-round. Reservations necessary. $-$$; credit cards not accepted. Call (423) 429-5704; write 250 Apple Valley Road, Sevierville, TN 37862; or visit www.charitcreek.com.

Wildwood Lodge Bed and Breakfast. TN-154, 3636 Pickett Park Highway. Guests will find Wildwood nestled between Pickett State Park and Big South Fork. The innkeepers are avid hikers and can steer you to trails or help you plan other outdoor adventures. Ten rooms, all with private baths, are complete with modern conveniences and decorated with unusual natural art, crafts, and pressed local wildflower pictures. A full country-style breakfast awaits guests, with treats such as wildflower honey, homemade preserves, and Mennonite molasses. A five-course candlelit dinner or a three-course evening supper is offered nightly with advance reservations, and a hot tub is available on the deck. A twenty-seven-stall stable means you can bring your own horses for riding. (Note: Wildwood Lodge is on central time and Big South Fork is on eastern time.) $$. (931) 879-9454; http://web/infoave.net/~wildwoodbed.

RUGBY

Just 18 miles east of Jamestown on TN–52 sits the historic English village of Rugby. Thomas Hughes, best known for his book *Tom Brown's Schooldays,* set out to start a new colony in the hills of the Cumberland Plateau back in 1880. During its heyday in the late nineteenth century, 450 residents populated the utopian community, most of them considered the cream of British society. But a typhoid epidemic, drought, disputed land titles, and a fire that destroyed Rugby's resort hotel caused the tiny town to fail.

It wasn't until the late 1960s that restoration began on some of the original structures. Today, about twenty Victorian-style buildings remain, many of which are virtually unchanged. Historic Rugby, Inc., conducts guided walking tours of four of the structures, and some you can explore by yourself. All are on the National Register of Historic Places.

WHERE TO GO

Tours begin at the Schoolhouse Visitor's Centre, which features exhibits and artifacts explaining the history of Rugby. The Thomas Hughes Library holds 7,000 original volumes of Victorian literature and is considered one of the most complete collections of its type in the United States. Visitors also can see Kingstone Lisle, Thomas Hughes's Gothic cottage, and Christ Church Episcopal, which has been used continuously for public worship since 1887. The 1849 rosewood organ is still played for services, which are open to the public every Sunday morning. Tours are conducted daily year-round, weather permitting.

Other buildings worth stopping at include the reconstructed Rugby Craft Commissary, which sells an assortment of local crafts and British food products. Rugby Printing Works is open most Saturdays and showcases nineteenth-century printing methods and techniques. Trails, many of which have been in use since Rugby's founding, lead to the Gentleman's Swimming Hole and the Clear Fork River.

Historic Rugby hosts four major events each year: the Festival of British and Appalachian Culture in May, the Pilgrimage of Homes every other August (the next one will be August 2005), Ghostly Gatherings in October, and Christmas at Rugby in early December (see "Festivals and Celebrations"). Traditional craft and art workshops also are held throughout the year.

The restored village caters to small and large groups and offers special interpretive programs as well. For more information, write Historic Rugby, Inc., P.O. Box 8, Rugby, TN 37733. Fee. (423) 628-2441; www.historicrugby.org.

WHERE TO SHOP

R. M. Brooks General Store. TN-52. This general store has served residents well over the years with basic groceries and supplies. Hornets' nests and snakeskins hang in the musty old building, which was built in 1930, and the counter holds a jar of bologna and a large hoop of cheddar cheese. Other historic memorabilia and crafts abound alongside necessary foodstuffs if you're in need. Open daily except Sunday. (423) 628-2533.

WHERE TO EAT

Harrow Road Cafe. Central Avenue and Harrow Road. This dining spot was built in 1985 but conforms to the architecture of the village's historic structures. The menu combines Cumberland Plateau country cooking with a few British specialties such as bangers and mash, shepherd's pie, and Welsh rarebit. The dense spoon rolls are a great way to start a meal. High ceilings, oil lamps, and dulcimer music make this cafe an enjoyable spot to dine. Open daily for breakfast and lunch; dinner served Friday and Saturday. $-$$. (423) 628-2350; www.historicrugby.org/dining/dining.htm.

WHERE TO STAY

Grey Gables Bed 'n Breakfast Inn. TN-52. Grey Gables, located 1 mile west of Rugby, opened in 1990 and combines country charm with modern conveniences. There are ten bedrooms, six baths, several sitting areas, two decks, a family room, and an 80-foot veranda, complete with rockers. A hearty country breakfast and full dinner are included in the price. Grey Gables hosts a variety of events throughout the year and on special weekends, so you might want to call ahead to see what's scheduled. $$$. (423) 628–5252; www.rugbytn.com.

Newbury House Bed and Breakfast. At the corner of Faringdon Road and Newbury Road. Here the cool mountain air and the drone of crickets will lull you to a slumber unencumbered by phones, television, and other city noises. Newbury House was the colony's first boarding house and has been restored with Victorian antiques and furnishings. There are six bedrooms, some with private baths, others with a shared bath, and a suite. Complimentary tea and coffee are served in the afternoon with some homemade sweets. Guests get a full breakfast at the Harrow Road Cafe as part of the price. Open year-round. $$. (423) 628–2441; www.historicrugby.org /lodging/lodging.htm.

Pioneer Cottage and Percy Cottage. These two cottages dating from the 1880s have been restored to accommodate tourists. Pioneer Cottage on TN–52 has three bedrooms, a bath and a half, a parlor, a screened-in back porch, and a fully furnished kitchen; it can sleep eight people. Linens are furnished and children are welcome. Percy Cottage's upstairs suite for overnight lodging sleeps three. Two bedrooms, a bath, a sitting area, and a kitchenette make the reconstructed (circa 1884) structure, located on Cumberland Avenue, a comfortable place to stay overnight. Open year-round. $$. (423) 628–2441; www.historicrugby.org/lodging/lodging.htm.

Note: Additional privately owned historic homes are often available to guests with prior arrangements. Contact Historic Rugby, Inc., for information at (423) 628–2441.

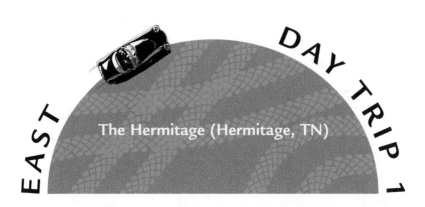

The Hermitage (Hermitage, TN)

THE HERMITAGE

To reach The Hermitage, take exit 8 off Briley Parkway and head out US-70 east, also called Lebanon Pike, passing through the community of Donelson. At the Old Hickory Boulevard intersection, turn north and travel about a mile until you reach The Hermitage. Or take I-40 east, get off at exit 221A, then head north 4 miles on Old Hickory Boulevard to the entrance.

Andrew Jackson, seventh president of the United States, came back to Tennessee after his years in the White House and made his home here. There are several areas to visit at The Hermitage, including a museum, the mansion, outbuildings and garden, Old Hermitage Church, and Tulip Grove. The grounds of The Hermitage took quite a beating during a tornado in 1998. In fact, more than 1,200 trees, including many cedars that used to line the path to the mansion, were lost. Some of them dated back to 1838. An enormous effort was made immediately following the storm to replant many of the trees, including the cedars.

The Hermitage is Middle Tennessee's first Smithsonian Institution affiliate, which gives The Hermitage access to the Smithsonian's vast collections through long-term loans of artifacts and other outreach services. For additional information, write to 4580 Rachel's Lane, Hermitage, TN 37076; call (615) 889-2941; or visit www.thehermitage.com.

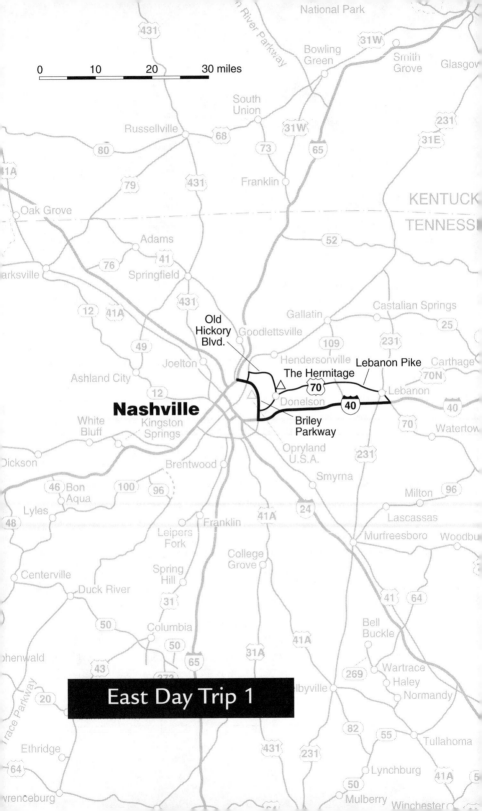

East Day Trip 1

WHERE TO GO

The best place to start your guided tour of The Hermitage is at the museum and mansion. Then you can get back in your car and drive down Rachel's Lane to Tulip Grove and Old Hermitage Church.

The museum gives visitors a look at some of the furnishings, silver, costumes, and other historic items from Jackson's day. Pieces of pottery unearthed by the archaeologists who work every summer excavating on the grounds are on view as well as paintings and photographs. The Brewster Carriage, which Jackson used in Washington and on trips between The Hermitage and Nashville, is also on display.

The mansion was built between 1819 and 1821 and is a fine example of Greek Revival–style architecture (a fire destroyed much of the original house in 1834, which was done in the Federal style). The modest structure, which is said to have more original furnishings than any other presidential home in the United States, is situated on 625 acres and was once a working farm of 1,100 acres with 150 slaves. As you enter the residence, it is the French wallpaper tracing a Greek legend that is most striking. The grand staircase, antique beds, and fireplace mantels are just a few of the dominant features in the two-story home. A major restoration project, completed in 1996, carefully replicated paints, wallpapers, and textiles.

Several outbuildings, including the kitchen, smokehouse, original cabins, and springhouse, show what life was like in Middle Tennessee in the early 1800s. Rachel's Garden, named after Jackson's beloved wife, is a beautiful site in the spring. Roses, irises, peonies, and herbs bloom alongside many other plants in the garden, which is located to one side of the mansion. In the back corner is the couple's tomb, adjacent to the graves of other family members. A magnolia tree that Jackson planted for his wife was also lost in a 1998 tornado.

A short drive down Rachel's Lane takes you to Tulip Grove, an 1836 Greek Revival home nestled in a grove of tulip poplars—the state tree. This was the residence of Andrew Jackson Donelson, Rachel's nephew and Jackson's secretary during his White House years.

Jackson built the Old Hermitage Church for his wife in 1823, and it became the place where the former president himself worshipped.

Fire claimed the original structure's roof and interior in 1965, but the building has since been restored. The nearby cemetery holds almost 500 graves of Confederate veterans and many members of the Donelson family.

The Hermitage is open daily except Thanksgiving, Christmas, and the third week of January. The church is open in the summer months only when volunteers are available. Guided tours of the garden are available April through October. During the summer, archaeology digs take place on the grounds, and the public is welcome to watch and ask questions. A farm tour, which gives visitors a glimpse into what the estate was like when it was a working farm, is also available. Fee. (615) 889-2941; www.hermitage.org.

WHERE TO SHOP

The Hermitage Museum Store. 4580 Rachel's Lane. Food products from around the state, crystal, antique jewelry, re-creations of presidential place settings, Iron Mountain stoneware, a wide variety of Tennessee crafts, and a large selection of books on gardening, history, and cooking make this store definitely worth a stop. It operates on the same schedule as the historic home. (615) 889-2941.

WHERE TO EAT

Café Monell's. 4580 Rachel's Lane. This bright cafeteria-style eatery features a meat-and-vegetable daily special, a variety of sandwiches, and homemade desserts. Family dining at Cabin-by-the-Spring is also offered, with choices such as fried chicken, pot roast, mashed potatoes, and corn pudding. Call ahead for reservations. Open daily for lunch as well as afternoon snacks and beverages. $$. (615) 889-2941.

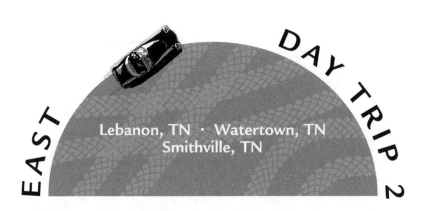

Lebanon, TN · Watertown, TN
Smithville, TN

LEBANON

From The Hermitage, you can continue on US-70 east to take in the small towns on this day trip. Lebanon certainly deserves a stop if you like antiques. Fifty dealers represented in shops around the old town square have named their hamlet the "Antique City of the South." Cuz's Antique Center, the Downtown Antique Mall, and Rainbow Relics are just a few of the shops where all sorts of treasures can be found. The stores are open daily for browsing. And don't miss the Outlet Village of Lebanon, where shoppers can find Coach, Brooks Brothers, Gap, Jones New York, and Nautica stores.

Lebanon is also the headquarters for Cracker Barrel Old Country Stores, which always satisfy road-hungry travelers with their well-prepared home-cooked meals. Cracker Barrel restaurants are located off interstates across the state and beyond. For more information about the area, stop at the Lebanon–Wilson County Chamber of Commerce, 149 Public Square; call (615) 444-5503; or visit www.wilsoncounty.com/lebanonchamber.

WATERTOWN

Stay on US-70 east for fifteen minutes and you'll see a sign for Historic Watertown, which has remained much the same since the early twentieth century. Cross over the railroad tracks and you'll reach the

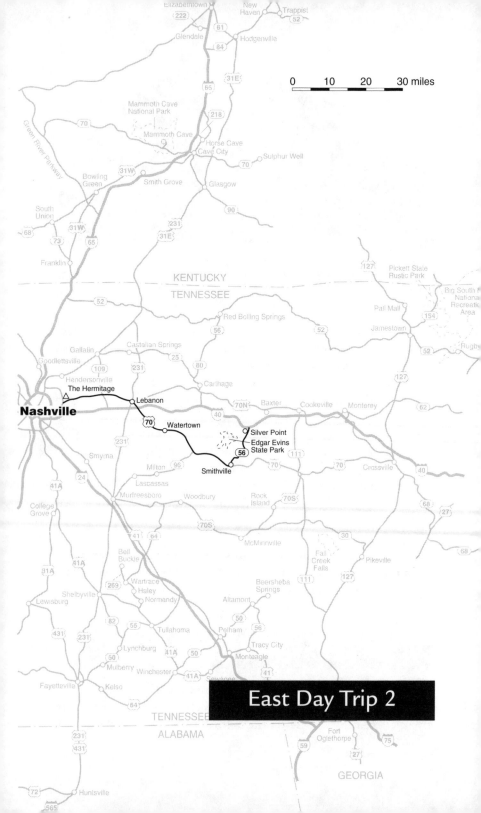

square, where several antiques stores surround a small gazebo. Here the pace is slow and the folks are friendly. They hold a Mile Long Yard Sale every April and October and a Jazz Festival in July (see "Festivals and Celebrations"). An Excursion Train heads to Watertown monthly from Nashville's Riverfront Park for shopping and eating or to attend one of the many festivals. Call Historic Watertown (615-237-9999) for a schedule of yearly events and more information on the train.

WHERE TO EAT

Charlie's. 406 Public Square. Located in a historic building downtown, Charlie's is a "meat-and-three" with good Southern food. Open for lunch and dinner daily, lunch only on Sunday. $-$$. (615) 237-9100.

　　The Depot Junction Cafe. 108 Depot Avenue. This restaurant's homemade biscuits and gravy, pancakes, and omelets can satisfy morning hunger pangs while the plate lunches, burgers, steaks, and seafood will fill up diners the rest of the day. Kids will enjoy the model train that runs above the dining room, and grown-ups might want to purchase some of the crafts and antique items that are for sale here. Open daily for all three meals, except Sunday, when you can come for breakfast or lunch. $-$$. (615) 237-3976.

　　Snow White. US-70 west. It's the biscuits that keep diners coming back for more here, the spot where locals gather for early morning conversation (Snow White opens at 5:00 A.M.). A lunch buffet also pleases, and items such as popcorn shrimp, hamburger steak, and barbecue greet guests at dinnertime (try the Friday night catfish buffet). Open for breakfast and lunch Monday through Friday; dinner served Monday through Saturday. $; credit cards not accepted. (615) 237-9715.

WHERE TO STAY

Watertown Bed & Breakfast. 116 Depot Street (right off the square). This historic railroad hotel, built in 1898, has five rooms for guests, all with private baths, and will do dinner parties for large groups and wedding receptions with advance notice. A full breakfast is provided, along with a tandem bike for those who want to explore the sleepy town. $$. (615) 237-9999; www.bbonline.com/tn/watertown.

SMITHVILLE

Continue down US-70 east a short distance and you will reach Smithville, which is synonymous with the Fiddlers' Jamboree, held the weekend before July 4 (see "Festivals and Celebrations"), and the Appalachian Center for Crafts. Smithville is convenient to Edgar Evins State Park (home to popular Center Hill Lake) and the scenic Burgess Falls State Natural Area, located between Smithville and Sparta, Tennessee.

WHERE TO GO

Smithville-DeKalb County Chamber of Commerce. 210 East Public Square (first floor of the courthouse). Stop here for brochures and information about the area. Open Monday through Friday. (615) 597-4163; www.smithvilletn.com or www.dekalbtn.com.

Appalachian Center for Crafts. 1560 Craft Center Drive (just across the Hurricane Bridge off TN-56). This nationally recognized craft center, a branch of the Tennessee Technological University in Cookeville, is situated on 500 wooded acres overlooking Center Hill Lake. The school operates a gallery here that showcases the work of Tennessee craftspeople as well as artisans from thirteen Appalachian states. Wonderful handcrafted items such as jewelry, baskets, pottery, and glass are for sale, and two exhibition areas display historic, regional, and national works. Summer and weekend workshops are open to the public, and children can participate in a variety of programs. The gallery hosts two special events each year—the Annual Celebration of Craft in April and an annual Holiday Festival, the weekend following Thanksgiving. Open daily except for Thanksgiving, the week between Christmas and New Year's Day, Easter, and two days at the end of June. Free summer tours of the artists' studios are offered, but call ahead for times. Free. (615) 597-6801; www.tntech.edu/craftcenter/index.htm.

Edgar Evins State Park. Route 1 off TN-56 (about 20 miles north of Smithville), Silver Point. This scenic park, built around Center Hill Lake, encompasses about 6,000 acres of steep walled bluffs and narrow ridges. Long ago the area served as a hunting ground for nearby tribes of Indians. The lake is a popular recre-

ation area, with its swimming, fishing, boating, and picnicking facilities, and the park offers tent and trailer campsites as well as
modern cabins overlooking the water. Free. (931) 858-2114;
www.state.tn.us/environment/parks/parks/edgarevins.

WHERE TO SHOP

Griffin's Fruit Market. US-70. If you want to munch on some
fresh fruit or bag some tomatoes to take home, stop at Griffin's.
Not only do the proprietors sell farm-fresh produce but honey, molasses, cider, and plants and garden seeds line the shelves during the
spring and summer months. Open daily. (615) 597-5030.

WHERE TO EAT

Simply Southern Restaurant. 930 West Broad Street. This downtown buffet-style eatery is popular with locals and is a regular
meeting place. Open for breakfast, lunch, and dinner daily. $$. (615)
597-6276.

    Sundance. 107 East Main Street. Homemade daily specials bring
folks into Sundance, where diners feast on baked chicken, Chinese
dishes, and even Mexican fare. Dinner consists of entrees such as
seafood, pasta, trout, prime rib, and catfish. You can walk out with
some natural foods and vitamins from the restaurant/shop, too, and
Sundance also caters. Open Tuesday through Friday for lunch;
dinner served on Friday and Saturday. $-$$. (615) 597-1910.

WHERE TO STAY

The Inn at Evins Mill. 1535 Evins Mill Road (off US-70). Tennessee
state senator Edgar Evins purchased this property in 1937, erecting
a 4,600-square-foot lodge on a bluff overlooking Fall Creek and the
mill. The coziness still beckons visitors with stone fireplaces, hardwood floors, and antiques. In addition, fourteen guest rooms, each
with private bath, are privy to the restful sound of the water.

    Guests to Evins Mill can fish for bass or bluegill in the pond, hike
wooded trails to Culcarmac Falls—a 90-foot cascading waterfall that
pools into a cool swimming hole—play board games, or just read a
book on one of the breezy porches. The inn accommodates corporate meetings, bed-and-breakfast guests, weddings, and other gatherings. A three-course, country-gourmet dinner is offered to

overnight guests as well as a full breakfast in the morning. Call about special theme weekends such as the Fourth of July, Halloween, and Valentine's Day. Children are welcome on select weekends, but parents should be mindful of the hilly nature of the surroundings. It's also wise to plan ahead and call for reservations. $$$. (615) 269-3740 or (800) 383-2349; www.evinsmill.com.

COOKEVILLE

Cookeville, which is a straight shot east from Nashville on I-40, is probably best known for Tennessee Technological University, which educates approximately 9,100 students annually. Cookeville has been pegged as one of America's top ten retirement places and was cited as the most economical city in the nation in 1995.

WHERE TO GO

Cookeville-Putnam County Chamber of Commerce. One Town Center, 1 West First Street. Stop here for more information about Cookeville. Open Monday through Friday. (800) 264–5541 or (931) 526–2211; www.cookevillechamber.com.

Arda Lee's Hidden Hollow. 1901 Mount Pleasant Road. Kids and adults alike can frolic in this eighty-six-acre playground. Fishing, hiking, swimming, volleyball, horseshoes, and a petting zoo will entertain children, and there are shelters to grill and picnic in. A treehouse, tepee, and multicolored fountain will also delight the little ones. Hidden Hollow is popular for family reunions, picnics, weddings, and birthday parties. It is open daily. Fee. (931) 526–4038.

Cookeville Depot Museum. Broad at Cedar. Railroad fans will enjoy the artifacts, old photographs, and other exhibits that pertain to the train days of another era (including a caboose with its original interior). The depot was built in 1909 and is noteworthy for its

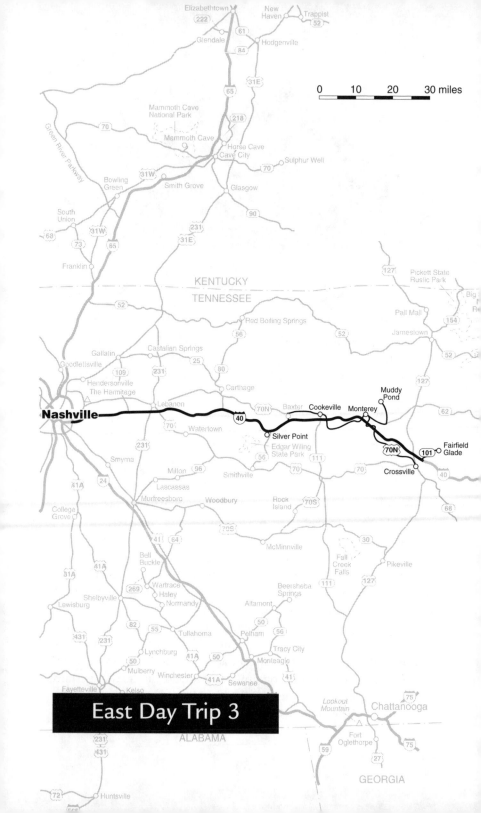

East Day Trip 3

unusual pagoda-style roofline and brick exterior. Open Tuesday through Saturday. Free. (931) 528-8570.

WHERE TO EAT

Crawdaddy's West Side Grill. 53 West Broad Street. This restaurant, which specializes in fresh Cajun-style cuisine, is located in Cookeville's historic West Side District near the Depot Museum. Lunch and dinner are served daily, and outdoor dining is available. $$$. (931) 526-4660.

Poet's on the Square. 230 East Broad Street. This coffee bar, which is adjacent to Bookworks, tempts diners looking for homemade muffins, pastries, desserts, teas, and gourmet coffee. The eatery also serves salads and is known for its panini sandwich (offered only on Tuesday and Thursday). Buy a book next door and read while you munch on some of the tasty treats. Regional artwork is for sale, and the coffee bar often has nightly entertainment and poetry readings. Open Monday through Saturday from early in the morning to late at night and Sunday afternoon. $. (931) 372-2201; www.poetscoffee.com.

Stroud's Barbeque. 1201 East Spring Street. Next door to the Food Lion, diners can stop by Stroud's for pork sandwiches, barbecued beef, ribs, smoked turkey and ham, and typical side orders such as baked beans, potato salad, and coleslaw. Lunch and dinner are served Monday through Saturday. $$; credit cards not accepted. (931) 528-7020.

WHERE TO STAY

Timber Ridge Inn and Jacuzzi Suites. 16300 Smithville Highway, Silver Point. Located just outside Putnam County but near Cookeville, the Timber Ridge Inn and Jacuzzi Suites is close to Interstate 40 and Center Hill Lake. Situated on twenty-five acres, the inn's grounds provide room to hike, or you can choose to stay inside in one of the inn's four rooms, two of which sport hot tubs. There's also a unit with a washer and dryer for longer stays. $$$. (931) 858-4032; www.n-sites.com/timberridgeinn.

MONTEREY

Monterey is about 13 miles due east from Cookeville. The small town is a good jumping-off spot for heading north to the communities of Jamestown and Rugby (see NORTHEAST, DAY TRIP 4).

WHERE TO GO

Muddy Pond Mennonite Community. TN-164 (about a fifteen-minute drive north from Monterey), Muddy Pond. The Mennonites in this small community continue the traditions of their ancestors by making harnesses and buggies. Visitors from around the state come each fall to see molasses making in action. A general store stocking Mennonite-made crafts, quilts, and natural food is located in the center of town, as is a bakery. Call (931) 445-7829 for the general store, or try the Cookeville-Putnam Convention and Visitors Bureau at (800) 264-5541.

WHERE TO STAY AND EAT

The Garden Inn. 1400 Bee Rock Road. Innkeepers Dickie and Stephanie Hinton have carved out a comfortable place for a weekend getaway. The inn, which was built in 1996, provides twelve rooms, with a view of either the gardens or the mountains. Perched on the edge of the Cumberland Plateau, the property has fifteen acres of gardens and grounds with a simulated mountain stream running through the building. The rooms all have private baths and walnut or cherry furnishings, and some have whirlpools or fireplaces. Breakfast varies from country to gourmet, with sinful sweets offered to guests before retiring. A large conference room is available for meetings. Dinner is available with advance reservations to large groups using the facility. $$$. The innkeepers raise their own vegetables and herbs and have blackberry, raspberry, and blueberry patches in addition to a small vineyard. $$-$$$. (931) 839-1400 or (888) 293-1444; www.thegardeninnbb.com.

CROSSVILLE

Crossville is the county seat for Cumberland County and was the site of a Subsistence Homestead project during the Depression. About 250 local families benefited from Franklin D. Roosevelt's program that attempted to aid the rural population during the Depression of the 1930s. Today many of the homes built then are still owned by former homesteaders. Many of the quaint stone cottages can be seen along US-127 south and TN-68 south.

WHERE TO GO

Greater Cumberland County Chamber of Commerce. 34 South Main Street. Stop here for brochures and maps to familiarize yourself with the area. Open Monday through Friday. (931) 484-8444; www.crossville-chamber.com.

Cumberland County Playhouse. US-70 (just west of downtown). This playhouse, which started in 1965, is one of the ten largest theaters in rural America in terms of audience served—some 145,000 patrons annually. The theater stages productions ranging from Broadway musicals to original plays based on Appalachian heritage on both indoor and outdoor stages. Open February through mid-December. Call for the current season's productions. Fee. (931) 484-5000; www.ccplayhouse.com.

Cumberland Mountain State Park. US-127 south. On top of the Cumberland Plateau (1,859 feet up), you will find a wooded park stretching over more than 1,500 acres. Hiking, tennis, fishing, golf, swimming, and boating are available, as are camping facilities—both tent and trailer. Many different types of cabins are available in the park, too, most of which have fireplaces and furnished kitchens. Hungry visitors can enjoy lunch and dinner at the large restaurant overlooking the lake. Open year-round. Free. Call (931) 484-6138 for cabin reservations or (931) 484-7186 for restaurant information; or visit www.state.tn.us/environment/parks/parks/CumberlandMtn/.

Homestead Tower Museum. US-127 south and TN-68 south (4 miles south of Crossville). This 80-foot octagonal tower, which formerly served as administrative offices, now houses a collection of photographs, documents, and artifacts depicting the Homestead project of FDR's New Deal administration. Visitors can climb to the observation room at the top of the structure for a view of some of the homesteads. Open daily. Closed mid-December through mid-March. Fee. (931) 456-9663.

Stonehaus Winery. 2444 Genesis Road (exit 320 at I-40). Stonehaus produces a small selection of wines, ranging from a Homestead White to a Muscadine. Tours show wine lovers the whole process, from crushing grapes to bottling. Try some of the homemade fudge here, too, and check out the Cheese Pantry, filled with more than forty varieties of cheese, bread, and gourmet foods. Picnic facilities are located on the grounds, as is Stonehaus Antiques and Gifts. Halcyon Days Restaurant is next door to the winery and is a great place for lunch or dinner (see "Where to Eat"). Open daily, but hours are cut back during winter. Free. (931) 484-9463; www.stonehauswinery.com.

WHERE TO SHOP

Crossville Depot Gifts. 14 North Street. This shop sells a variety of gifts, including special teas, chocolates, candies, and coffees. Open Monday through Saturday. (931) 456-2586; www.crossvilleonline .com/Businesses/GiftShops/Depot/.

Cumberland General Store. 1 Highway 68 (just outside of town, across from Homestead Tower). Claiming to sell "Goods in Endless Variety for Man and Beast," this general store offers a fascinating assortment—twig chairs, wine-making supplies, oil lamps, water pumps, tools, remedies, cast-iron cookware, toiletries, and dry goods are just a few of the items available. For a small fee, you can take home Cumberland's mail-order catalog detailing the store's unusual wares. Open daily year-round, except on Sunday from January through mid-March. (931) 484-8481; www.cumberlandgeneral.com/.

Factory Stores of America. 361 Sweeny Drive (exit 320 off I-40). Bargain hunters may want to browse through the many stores here, including Van Heusen, Bass Shoes, Dress Barn, Kitchen Collection, Corning/Revere, and Fieldcrest Cannon. Open daily. (931) 484-7165.

Simonton's Cheese House. 2278 Highway 127 south. Since 1947, this popular specialty shop has been known for its famous medium cheddar cheese hoop. There's a large selection of cheeses, gourmet foods, seasonings, and pastas to browse through, and Simonton's ships its mail-order products all over the world. Open daily. (931) 484-5193 or (888) 819-3226; www.simontonscheese.com.

WHERE TO EAT

Halcyon Days Restaurant. 2444 Genesis Road (next door to Stonehaus Winery). This white-tablecloth dining spot serves creative pasta dishes, stuffed quail, fresh seafood, and steaks and has a full wine list (including some from Stonehaus). A separate lounge area complements the restaurant. Reservations suggested for dinner. Open for lunch and dinner Monday through Saturday. $$-$$$. (931) 456-3663.

Toy's Family Restaurant. US-127 south. Boasting country cooking and Southern hospitality, this casual restaurant serves up daily blue-plate specials in addition to regular selections of country ham, biscuits and gravy, and home-baked pies. Open Monday through Saturday. $; credit cards not accepted. (931) 484-9819.

WHERE TO STAY

Several resort communities in the Crossville area offer accommodations and dining, golfing, fishing, horseback riding, and other recreational activities. Call the Chamber of Commerce for a complete listing at (931) 484-8444.

Fairfield Glade Resort. Peavine Road (exit 322 off I-40), Fairfield Glade. If you want the amenities of a large resort community, stay at the 12,700-acre Fairfield Glade, located about 10 miles from Crossville. With a guest card from the one-hundred-room, two-level lodge, you can enjoy tennis courts, swimming pools, a miniature golf course, nearly a dozen boating and fishing lakes, five full golf courses (four are for members and one is public), horseback riding, hiking trails, and other resort facilities. Three restaurants also operate on the premises, and guests can stay in villa or condominium units as well. $$. (931) 484-3723; www.fairfieldglade.org.

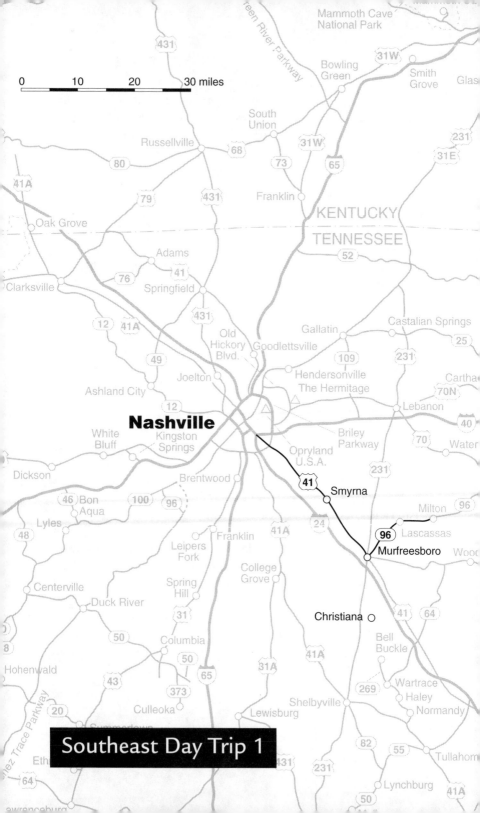

Southeast Day Trip 1

SMYRNA

To get to Smyrna, head down US–41/70S for about 15 miles. When Nissan Motor Manufacturing Corporation U.S.A. began producing trucks here in 1983, the company transformed Smyrna from a tiny hamlet to the first automobile factory for Nissan in the United States. The small community and surrounding area were also important during the Civil War.

WHERE TO GO

Nissan North America Inc. 983 Nissan Drive. Nissan is the county's largest employer and now produces both light trucks and automobiles at this 5.1-million-square-foot plant. Public tours are offered on Tuesday. (615) 459-1444.

Sam Davis Home. 1399 Sam Davis Road. This 168-acre plantation is indicative of the middle-class lifestyle in antebellum Middle Tennessee. The circa 1810 home with an addition from the 1840s, was owned by Sam Davis, a Civil War hero who chose to hang rather than reveal information to the Union forces. The two-story clapboard residence, which has been on tour since 1930, features many of the Davis family's original furnishings. Guided tours are offered of the home and grounds, and a small museum displays family and war memorabilia. The house has no air-conditioning, and there are several steps to navigate. Open daily except certain holidays. Fee. (615) 459-2341; www.samdavishome.org.

WHERE TO EAT

Omni Hut. US–41 south. For more than forty-two years, this Polynesian/Chinese eatery has been serving up ethnic specialties to area residents. Try the Tahitian Feast to sample a variety of dishes, or opt for the grilled kebabs. You can also choose to bring your own wine to this smoke-free restaurant. Open Tuesday through Saturday for dinner. $–$$. (615) 459–4870; www.omnihut.com.

Rossi's Restaurant. 114 Front Street. Stop by Rossi's for Italian specialties such as grinders, pasta, calzones, pizza, and entrees that range from shrimp scampi to veal and peppers. Open for lunch Monday through Friday; dinner served Monday through Saturday. $–$$. (615) 459–7992.

MURFREESBORO

Continue down US–41 south for about 12 miles to reach Murfreesboro. The 600-acre campus of Middle Tennessee State University (MTSU) is a prominent part of life in this city, entertaining residents with a variety of concerts, art shows, and theater productions throughout the year. Just a mile from downtown is the geographic center of Tennessee, so determined in 1834. Now a stone obelisk marks the spot. Murfreesboro, like many Tennessee cities, has several antiques stores for those who like to collect, and area dealers stage an antiques show and sale in July every year on the MTSU campus (see "Festivals and Celebrations").

Each August, the International Grand Championship Walking Horse Show brings top champion horses to compete in Murfreesboro (see "Festivals and Celebrations").

WHERE TO GO

Rutherford County Chamber of Commerce. 501 Memorial Boulevard. The chamber has a twenty-four-hour welcome center outside offering brochures and information about the area; open Monday through Friday. (615) 893–6565; www.rutherford chamber.org.

Cannonsburgh Village. 312 South Front Street. The first buildings in this reconstructed pioneer village appeared in 1974 as an

American Revolution Bicentennial project. Visitors to Cannonsburgh—the original name of Murfreesboro—can see a blacksmith shop, gristmill, chapel, country store, and other structures reminiscent of early Southern life. The self-guided walking tour also includes the "world's largest red cedar bucket," a 2,000-gallon container made in Murfreesboro in 1887. Each July, Cannonsburgh is the site for Uncle Dave Macon Days, an old-time musical celebration (see "Festivals and Celebrations"). Open Tuesday through Sunday from May through mid-December. Free, but guided tours are available for a fee. (615) 890-0355.

Center for the Arts. 110 West College Street. This structure was originally built as a post office in 1909 but was converted to an art gallery and performance hall in 1995. The center is home to the Murfreesboro Little Theatre, the Stones River Chamber Players, and various traveling productions and is a venue for rotating art exhibits. Open Tuesday through Saturday. Free. (615) 904-2787.

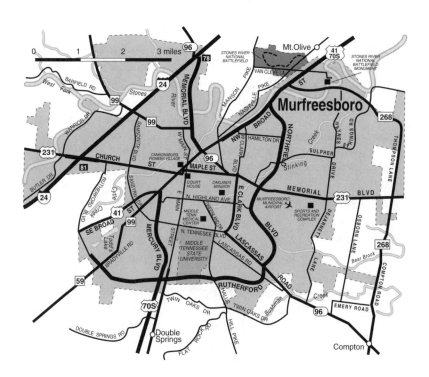

The Discovery Center at Murfree Spring. 502 Southeast Broad Street. The Children's Discovery House moved in 2002 to an 18,000-square-foot facility that features a terrific array of hands-on exhibits for children to enjoy. There are also twenty acres of wetland habitat where kids can discover plants and animals in a natural setting. The Discovery Center offers a variety of activities each month and also has Museum-to-Go programs for area schools. Fee. (615) 890-2300; www.discoverycenteronline.org.

Oaklands Historic House Museum. 900 North Maney Avenue. This attractive historic home, built between 1820 and 1860, was once one of the most elegant plantations in Middle Tennessee. Oaklands served as a crucial site during the Civil War, with both Northern and Southern armies camping on its 1,500 acres. Guided tours include the mansion. The museum offers a variety of educational programs and the facility's Maney Hall can be rented for events. Open Tuesday through Sunday. Closed major holidays. Fee. (615) 893-0022; www.oaklandsmuseum.org.

Rutherford County Courthouse. Court House Square. This courthouse, with its distinctive clock tower, is one of six pre–Civil War buildings still in use in the state. There is a monument on the square dedicated to General Griffith Rutherford, a Revolutionary War officer for whom the county was named. A walking tour of the Public Square and East Main Street showcases some of the Neoclassic, Italianate, and Victorian buildings (get a brochure from the chamber of commerce). A number of shops and restaurants flourish on the square, which makes for a nice place to stroll. Open Monday through Friday. Free. (615) 898-7745.

Stones River National Battlefield. 3501 Old Nashville Highway (off US-41). This 450-acre national park was the site of one of the bloodiest battles of the Civil War, where more than 23,000 soldiers lost their lives. The visitor center contains a small museum and orientation program, along with a good selection of books about the war. The self-guided tour of the battlefield is done with an audiotape in your car. The Hazen Brigade Monument, erected in 1863 and said to be the oldest intact Civil War memorial in the country, is located here, as is Fortress Rosecrans, the largest earthen fort of its kind built during the war. The fortress, which visitors can walk through, was completed in 1863 as a supply depot for the Union drive south.

More than 6,000 soldiers rest in Stones River National Cemetery. Artillery and infantry demonstrations and other programs are scheduled throughout the summer. Open daily except Christmas Day. Free. (615) 893-9501; www.nps.gov/stri.

Stones River Greenway Trail. Fortress Rosecrans in Old Fort Park (exit 78B, off I-24). This 4½-mile trail is a place to walk, bicycle, or skate and enjoy nature. Interpretive exhibits enhance travels along the trail, which follows the scenic Stones River. One section connects Thompson Lane and Fortress Rosecrans while the other joins the Fortress with Cannonsburgh. Free. (615) 890-5333.

WHERE TO SHOP

Old Time Pottery. 480 River Rock Boulevard (exit 78 off I-24). For a tremendous variety of dinnerware, flatware, crystal, glass, and floral and craft supplies, look no further than this popular store. Other items include rugs, wallpaper, baskets, sheets, towels, mirrors, and cookware, all at discount prices. Open daily. (615) 890-6060.

Stones River Mall. 1720 Old Fort Parkway (exit 78 off I-24). This large mall includes a food court with various restaurants as well as shops such as Dillard's, Gap, American Eagle, and Victoria's Secret. Open daily. (615) 896-4486.

WHERE TO EAT

The City Cafe. 113 East Main Street. This popular eatery, known for its plate lunches served with billowing yeast rolls or corn sticks, has been catering to residents for more than one hundred years and has always been located on the downtown square. Try the fried chicken, and then finish your meal with one of the many delicious homemade pies. Open for breakfast, lunch, and dinner Monday through Saturday. $. (615) 893-1303.

The Front Porch Cafe. 114 East College Street. For sandwiches and soups, head to this nonsmoking restaurant, located inside a restored old home. The Front Porch's calling card is freshly made desserts, which change daily. Open for lunch Monday through Saturday; Friday night buffet. $$. (615) 896-6771.

Miller's Grocery. 7011 Main Street, Christiana. This popular restaurant is a bit outside of Murfreesboro but well worth the short drive. You'll find a terrific old country store atmosphere and

Southern comfort food here. Open for lunch Tuesday through Sunday; dinner Friday and Saturday by reservation. There's also live music on Friday and Saturday nights and a special buffet lunch on Sunday. Miller's caters as well. $–$$. (615) 893–1878; www.millers grocery.com.

WHERE TO STAY

Byrn-Roberts Inn. 346 East Main Street. This large inn is within walking distance of the historic downtown and includes a nice courtyard with a waterfall, which provides a nice spot for enjoying a cup of coffee or breakfast. The four guest rooms in this circa 1900 house all have a 12-foot ceiling, private bath, working fireplace, TV with cable, and private phone. A gourmet breakfast is served, and there's also a complimentary social hour with appetizers in the evening. $$$. (615) 867–0308; www.byrn-roberts-inn.com/.

Carriage Lane Inn and Reception House. 411 North Maney Avenue. Built in 1899 and extensively renovated in 1997, this pretty inn has three rooms, all with private baths, and a cottage that sleeps eight to ten. A full hearty breakfast is on tap in the morning for overnight guests. The Reception House nearby is available for parties or weddings and accommodates up to 250. No children or pets, but children are accepted when the entire house is reserved. $$$. (615) 890–3630; www.carriagelaneinn.com.

McMinnville, TN
Fall Creek Falls
State Resort Park (Pikeville, TN)

McMINNVILLE

To get to McMinnville, take US-70S east for approximately 45 miles. You'll pass through the rural town of Woodbury, which has an art center that draws visitors from around the area for its plays, art shows, and other events.

McMinnville is known as the "Nursery Capital of the World" due to its more than 450 nurseries that specialize in all types of trees, plants, and shrubs. Most of them are open on weekends.

WHERE TO GO

McMinnville–Warren County Chamber of Commerce. 110 South Court Square. Stop here for brochures and information about the area. Open Monday through Friday. (931) 473-6611; www.warrentn.com.

Cumberland Caverns. 1437 Cumberland Caverns Road (off Highway 8). Cumberland Caverns, which opened to the public in 1956, is one of Tennessee's largest caves. Ninety-minute guided tours take visitors into this U.S. National Landmark's underground world, with stalactites, pools, waterfalls, columns, and a light show with Christian overtones. The "Hall of the Mountain King" is the largest cave room east of the Mississippi River, measuring 600 feet long by 150 feet wide by 140 feet high. It has a dining room (by reservation only for parties of 40 or more) that seats 500 and is adorned with a

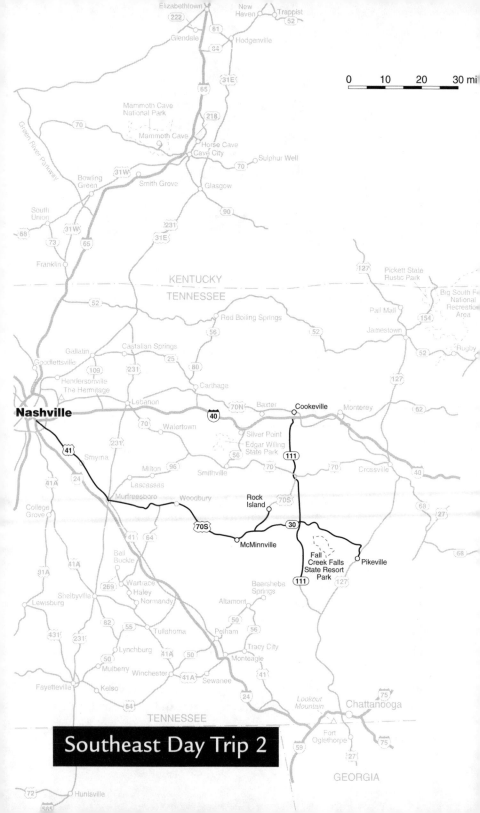

Southeast Day Trip 2

three-quarter-ton crystal chandelier. Bring a jacket—the cave temperature is about fifty-six degrees. Open daily from May 1 through October 31; by appointment from November through April. Fee. (931) 668-4396; www.cumberlandcaverns.com.

Rock Island State Park. Rock Island (14 miles northeast of McMinnville). The 883-acre park is located at the falls of the Caney Fork River near McMinnville. The scenic area is known for Great Falls, which cascades down the rocky hillside, and for the Spring Castle, an enchanting stone castle nestled in a lush glen (and a popular spot for weddings). In addition, there is camping, a natural sand beach with swimming, boating, fishing, tennis courts, basketball court, and picnic facilities. Ten cabins and a launch ramp onto Center Hill Lake are also located here. Fee. (931) 686-2471 or (800) 713-6065; www.state.tn.us/environment/parks/parks/RockIsland/.

WHERE TO STAY

Historic Falcon Manor. 2645 Faulkner Springs Road. This large mansion dates from 1896 and once served as a hospital. The present owners have restored the 10,000-square-foot structure and offer four guest suites on the grounds, but the emphasis is on tours. A full gourmet breakfast is served in the morning to overnight guests. A gift shop is also on the property, and a tea room serves lunch daily. Falcon Manor was recognized in 1997 by the National Trust for Historic Preservation. Guided tours are offered daily for a nominal fee. $$-$$$. (931) 668-4444; www.falconmanor.com.

FALL CREEK FALLS STATE RESORT PARK

From McMinnville, take TN-30 east to get to the north entrance of the park, or you can follow TN-30 to the TN-111 junction, then head south to get to the park. A quicker route from Nashville is to take I-40 to Cookeville, then go south on TN-111.

This state park, the largest in the system, offers some of the most spectacular scenery in Tennessee. Visitors can see majestic cascades, deep chasms and gorges, virgin timber, and the magnificent Fall Creek

Falls, which plunges 256 feet into a shaded pool. The falls is the highest waterfall east of the Rocky Mountains. The park is a popular destination for hiking and camping, and other amenities include an Olympic-size swimming pool, wading pool for children, boating facilities, an eighteen-hole golf course, tennis courts, ball fields, picnic grounds, bicycle paths, horse stables and trails, playgrounds, nature center, and rental bikes. Special events are scheduled throughout the year and include runs, backpacking trips, bicycle excursions, rock-climbing workshops, and craft shows. Twenty two-bedroom cabins are located here as well as ten three-bedroom, two-bath villas. There are also two group lodges. For camping reservations call (800) 250–8611; for other information call (423) 881–3297; or visit www.state.tn.us/environment/parks/parks/FallCreekFalls.

WHERE TO STAY AND EAT

Fall Creek Falls Bed & Breakfast Inn. Route 3, Box 298-B (1 mile from the north entrance to Fall Creek Falls State Resort Park), Pikeville. This modern brick-and-frame home provides seven guest rooms and one two-room suite, which are adorned with Victorian and country furnishings. In addition, there are three dining areas, a glassed-in Florida room, and three sitting areas. There is also a one-bedroom cabin for two. Overnighters will want to visit the gardens that grow in the five-acre yard, which also has a few picnic tables. Treats such as cinnamon rolls, breakfast burritos, and strawberry bread are offered in the morning, and lunch is available as long as the order is placed the night before. $$–$$$. (423) 881–5494; www.fallcreekfalls.com.

Fall Creek Falls Inn and Restaurant. Route 3, Pikeville. The modern inn and restaurant are situated on scenic Fall Creek Falls Lake. There are 144 rooms (a new building added 72 more rooms and a convention center in 1998, and the old building was refurbished), most with a private balcony or patio overlooking the lake. A large suite with kitchenette is also available. The restaurant offers three buffet-style meals in the attractive dining room as well as a full menu ($$). The inn can accommodate conferences, banquets, and other group gatherings. There is also a recreation room, fitness equipment, and shuffleboard here. Reservations should be made well in advance. $$. (800) 250–8610 or (423) 881–5241.

MONTEAGLE

To reach Monteagle from Murfreesboro (see SOUTHEAST DAY TRIP 1), take US–41 south for about 40 miles. Then it's a short drive up the mountain on US–41 to Monteagle; if you're heading here from Nashville, it's a straight shot down I-24 east (exit 134). This quaint community is situated atop the southern end of the scenic Cumberland Plateau. Monteagle is known mainly for its century-old Monteagle Sunday School Assembly, where families have made their summer homes for generations, and for the treacherous stretch of I-24 that winds up Monteagle Mountain. The interstate is particularly dangerous during the winter months because of its steep grade. Monteagle sits at the top of the incline, at an elevation of 2,100 feet.

Nashvillians like to escape to the area for the cool weather, great hiking at South Cumberland State Recreation Area, and the tranquility of the Assembly Grounds.

WHERE TO GO

Monteagle Assembly Grounds. US–41A/64 (exit 134 off I-24). The Assembly Grounds has a rich history as a cultural learning center, providing speakers, lecturers, and other programs to members of the interdenominational community and visitors during an eight-week season in the summer. This Chautauqua program is one of only four

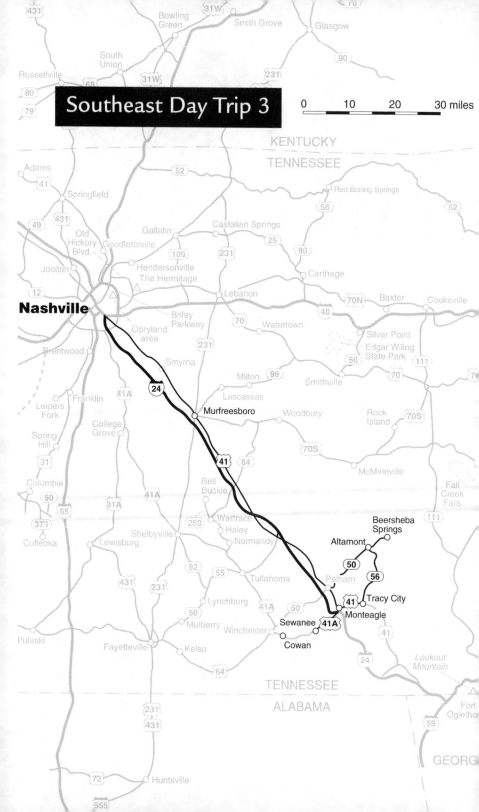

Southeast Day Trip 3

remaining programs of its type in the United States. For a modest daily fee, both adults and children can participate in the summer programs as well as use the pool and tennis facilities. Movies are shown in the auditorium in the evenings, and there are recreational activities for children.

During the rest of the year, families from around the area escape from the cities to spend leisurely weekends in the cool mountain retreats. Walking the grounds to admire the lovely homes, many of which date back to the 1890s, is worth an hour or two. There also is a bed-and-breakfast inn on the grounds (see "Where to Stay").

South Cumberland State Recreation Area. US–41A/56. The nine different entrances to the South Cumberland State Recreation Area stretch across the rugged terrain of the Cumberland Plateau. You can spend time hiking the hundreds of miles of trails and find unique rock formations, deep river gorges, waterfalls, and caves in the area's 12,700 acres.

Don't miss the Sewanee Natural Bridge, which was weathered from solid sandstone and stands 27 feet high. Other popular hiking spots include Fiery Gizzard Trail, which is one of the most difficult trails in the state, and the Savage Gulf State Natural Area, known for the 150-foot-deep crevice called Great Stone Door. Primitive camping at selected sites is available. The park visitor center is on US–41A/56, between Monteagle and Tracy City. Free. (931) 924–2980; www.state.tn.us/environment/parks/parks/SouthCumberland/.

WHERE TO SHOP

Mountain Outfitters. 808 West Main Street. Forget catalog shopping. You can find merchandise from Lands' End, Eddie Bauer, Banana Republic, J. Crew, and L.L.Bean at this small store (and all at a discount). Backpacks, hiking boots, ragg socks, and other outdoor gear are stocked here, too. Open daily. (931) 924–4100.

WHERE TO EAT

Blue Water Lodge. 903 West Main Street. This large casual dining spot is great for barbecue, fresh fish, and steaks. It's family-friendly, too, with a special menu for the little ones. Live music is often scheduled on the weekends. $–$$. (931) 924–7020.

WHERE TO EAT AND STAY

Jim Oliver's Smoke House. US–41A. This Southern-style restaurant's all-you-can-eat buffet for lunch and dinner features the Smoke House's famous hickory-smoked meats and pit barbecue. In addition, diners can choose among catfish, Southern fried chicken, sandwiches, and pizza. Cakes, pies, and cookies from the restaurant's in-house bakery beckon to visitors with a sweet tooth. Open daily for breakfast, lunch, and dinner. $–$$.

The Smoke House also has fourteen rustic cabins and the newly-remodeled Smoke House Lodge, a Best Western property with eighty-five rooms. $$$. (931) 924–2268; www.thesmokehouse.com.

WHERE TO STAY

Staying at one of the two bed-and-breakfast establishments on the Assembly Grounds is convenient for seeing the entire area and makes for a relaxing night away from home.

Adams-Edgeworth Inn. Monteagle Assembly Grounds (US–41A/56). This charming twelve-room inn is listed on the National Register of Historic Places and provides pleasant antiques-filled quarters with private baths and a well-stocked library for idling away the evening. A full breakfast greets guests in the morning in the cozy dining room, and the front-porch rockers provide a comfy spot for relaxing. The Adams-Edgeworth offers a five-course dinner during the week, and an elegant three-course meal Sunday through Tuesday nights. All require advance reservations. $$$. Special weekends are scheduled throughout the year, too. Open all year. $$$. (931) 924–4000 or (877) 352–9466; www.relaxinn.com.

Monteagle Inn. US–41A/56. Opened in 1997, this inn has modern amenities with a nod toward the past. Thirteen guest rooms, all with private baths, and a full breakfast pamper visitors. There's also a hot tub available in the courtyard, and a conference room for meetings. The inn offers cooking classes and has honeymoon and anniversary specials. $$$. (931) 924–3869; www.monteagleinn.com/.

SEWANEE

Sewanee is 6 miles west of Monteagle on US-41A/56. Indians named this mountain plateau, which now is a small college town centered around The University of the South, a well-respected school started by the leaders of the Episcopal Church.

WHERE TO GO

The University of the South. US-41A. This picturesque mountaintop campus was founded in 1857 and is worth seeing for its Gothic sandstone buildings inspired by Oxford University in England. Guerry Hall houses the university's art gallery and the auditorium, where summer concerts from the Sewanee Music Festival take place (see "Festivals and Celebrations"). Tours of the campus are available by appointment year-round. Carillon concerts entertain visitors on Sunday afternoon throughout the year. Free. (931) 598-1286; www.sewanee.edu/ssmf/.

WHERE TO SHOP

The Lemon Fair. 60 University Avenue. This quaint house is the place to buy locally made pottery, jewelry, stained glass, baskets, gourmet coffee, and T-shirts. Open Monday through Saturday. (931) 598-5248.

WHERE TO EAT

The Blue Chair Bakery and Coffee Shop. 41 University Avenue. This bright and cheerful bakery/coffeehouse/restaurant serves a fabulous breakfast and lunch, and you can't leave without tasting one of their terrific baked goods. The cakes are marvelous. Open Monday through Friday for breakfast, lunch, and afternoon snacks; breakfast and lunch only on Saturday. $. (931) 598-5434; www.the bluechair.com.

    Pearl's Foggy Mountain Cafe. 15344 Sewanee Highway (between Sewanee and Monteagle). Everything at Pearl's is made from scratch, local when available, organic when possible, and certainly fresh. Smoked salmon corn cakes, Brunswick stew, black beans and rice, roast stuffed pork, smoked trout, and green herb pesto pasta are but a few of the delicious choices diners can make at this creative eatery. Open for dinner daily and Sunday brunch. Reservations recommended. $$–$$$. (931) 598-9568.

Shenanigans. 12595 Sollace Freemen Highway. This popular restaurant is housed in an old timber-frame building that once served as a general store. Try one of the sandwiches, which come on homemade bread, or opt for pizza or a specialty grill item. Homemade soups and desserts also tempt diners, and the beer, served in Mason jars, is always cold. A gallery of pottery and fiber arts is also located inside. Open daily for lunch and dinner. $. (931) 598-5774.

WHERE TO STAY

The Franklin-Pearson House. 108 East Cumberland Street, Cowan. Cowan is located a short 7 miles "down the mountain" from Sewanee. The Franklin-Pearson House, which opened in 2003, is a nine-room bed-and-breakfast located in a restored railroad hotel. Guest rooms feature private baths, tasteful decor, and modern amenities. Both hot and cold breakfast items are served in the downstairs lobby. $$$. (931) 969-3223; www.franklinpearson.com.

TRACY CITY

To get to Tracy City, you'll have to backtrack through Monteagle, and then continue for 5 miles on US-41A/64. Tracy City and surrounding Grundy County were settled by a group of Swiss immigrants in 1870, and their influence still pervades the area today.

WHERE TO GO

Dutch Maid Bakery. 111 Main Street. Tennessee's oldest family-owned bakery, operating since 1902, offers visitors a step back in time. Founded by Swiss immigrants, the Dutch Maid sells delicious sourdough, raisin, pumpernickel, salt-rising, and other tasty breads; cakes, fruitcakes, and pastries; hard candies and licorice; plus a small selection of local crafts and honey. The bakery also offers a mail-order service. Open daily except Thanksgiving and Christmas. (931) 592-3171; www.dutch-maid.com.

BEERSHEBA SPRINGS

From Tracy City, go north on TN-56 for about 15 miles to reach Altamont. Then take TN-50 for about 5 miles to reach the old resort town of Beersheba Springs. In the 1800s the Beersheba Springs Hotel was the place to bed down for the night and get an evening meal—the "queen of all mineral resorts in Tennessee." More than a century later, the hotel still stands and is now owned by the United Methodist Church Assembly and used for summer meetings and retreats. Each August, however, the hotel is open to the public as the backdrop for an arts and crafts festival featuring about 250 exhibitors from several different states (see "Festivals and Celebrations"). (931) 779-3462.

Southeast Day Trip 4

CHATTANOOGA

You can take US-41 south through Murfreesboro to get to Chattanooga, but it's an easy and picturesque drive down I-24 to the river city and will take a little more than two hours. The route even takes you into Georgia for about 4 miles and then you're back in Tennessee. Even though you get to Lookout Mountain before Chattanooga, it's just as easy to head up the mountain after settling into Chattanooga first.

This railroad city is Tennessee's fourth largest and became immortalized in a popular song, "Chattanooga Choo Choo," because of its history as a major rail center. It also was home to the first Coca-Cola bottling plant in the world, opened in 1899 by two attorneys who paid $1.00 for the franchise rights. Those tiny hamburgers from Krystal were first fried here, and everybody's favorite Moon Pies are made in this Southeastern city. The University of Tennessee at Chattanooga has a nice campus with a variety of entertainment offered throughout the year.

A free downtown shuttle runs daily from the Tennessee Aquarium to the Chattanooga Choo Choo Holiday Inn, making stops at every block in between. Look for the blue, yellow, and red stop signs to catch an easy ride around downtown. (The Holiday Inn offers free parking.) You also can take historical and architectural tours of several sections of the downtown area. Stop by the visitor center, call the Convention and Visitors Bureau at (800) 322-3344 or (423)

756–8687, or visit www.chattanoogafun.com.

This area of the state is beautiful during autumn, and an annual Fall Color Cruise and Folk Festival spotlights the changing foliage in October (see "Festivals and Celebrations"). Chattanooga's location on a bend in the Tennessee River among the surrounding mountains makes it a scenic place to spend some time. And nearby Raccoon Mountain and Signal Mountain offer entertaining options for the family, from hang gliding and bungee jumping to go-carts and underground caverns. The Chattanooga area is on eastern time.

WHERE TO GO

Chattanooga Visitors Center. 2 Broad Street. This center, which is adjacent to the Tennessee Aquarium, is the place to get information about Chattanooga and the immediate area. Another visitor center operates in Hamilton Place mall. Open daily except Thanksgiving and Christmas. Free. (800) 322–3344 or (423) 756–8687; www.chattanoogafun.com.

Tennessee Aquarium. 1 Broad Street. Chattanooga hit pay dirt when the downtown aquarium opened in 1992, attracting more than one million visitors annually. The underwater museum is a big draw and with good reason. It's the first and largest freshwater aquarium in the world and home to more than 9,000 animals, including more than 350 species of fish, reptiles, amphibians, birds, and mammals. The attractive building sits right on the Tennessee

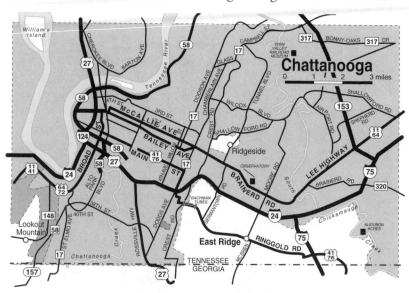

River downtown and is surrounded by Ross's Landing Park and Plaza, which is an interesting place to stroll before heading inside the $45-million structure. Architects cleverly designed the space so visitors are escalated up to the fourth floor and then make their way down by seeing all of the different areas of the aquarium.

Nickajack Lake, which can be seen on several levels, holds 138,000 gallons of water and is one of the largest freshwater tanks in the world. Particularly fascinating is "Rivers of the World," which displays fish from the Amazon, St. Lawrence, and Yenisey Rivers. Visitors can often see divers feeding the stingrays in the Gulf of Mexico exhibit. (There are scheduled dives November through February, during which the underwater divers will talk to visitors.) Books, toys, and all kinds of gifts and accessories are for sale in the gift shop on the first level, and there's also a folk art gallery. *Parents take note:* During peak times no strollers are allowed in the facility, but backpacks are provided for children under twenty-five pounds. The aquarium is wheelchair-accessible. A time-ticketed system helps with the crowds, but the aquarium is always busy.

Open daily except for Thanksgiving and Christmas, with extended hours on weekends from Memorial Day through Labor Day. Fee. (Children under three free, and combination tickets for the aquarium, IMAX 3-D Theater, and Creative Discovery Museum are offered at the ticket booths adjacent to the aquarium.) Behind-the-scenes tours give visitors a peek at the inner workings of a world-class aquarium. (800) 262-0695 or (423) 265-0695; www.tnaqua.org.

IMAX 3-D Theater. 201 Chestnut Street. An IMAX 3-D Theater opened in 1996, adding another dimension to the aquarium experience. Visitors can see a variety of exciting 3-D films, all played out on a six-story-high screen in a 400-seat theater. The Environmental Learning Lab is housed here, too, where kids can do some high-tech hands-on exploration. Large groups must call in advance to schedule free two-hour blocks of time on the computers, complete with guides who will answer questions and offer help (no admission fee). The IMAX shows films on the hour, with the last show stretching into the evening hours. Fee. (800) 262-0695 or (423) 265-0695.

Ross's Landing Park and Plaza. 100 Broad Street. This unique public space surrounding the Tennessee Aquarium blends history, native plants, and interesting landscape architecture. Chronological bands mark events that have shaped Chattanooga, such as the Civil War, the Trail of Tears, railroad history, the world's first Coca-Cola bottling plant, and the career of blues queen Bessie Smith, a Chattanooga native. Pick up a brochure in the visitor center located here that explains all of the significant time bands. Open daily. Live entertainment is scheduled periodically spring through fall. Public restrooms available. Free. (800) 322-3344.

The Chattanooga African-American Museum/Bessie Smith Hall. 200 East Martin Luther King Boulevard. The museum contains a collection of African art, musical recordings, blues queen Bessie Smith's original piano, a library with books and documents related to African Americans and their contributions to the growth of Chattanooga and the nation, and a small gift shop specializing in Afrocentric gifts. The center also houses Bessie Smith Hall, which features a small exhibit tracing the singer's life and career, music rooms for aspiring performers, educational programs, a research library on blues and jazz music, and a 260-seat cabaret-style performance hall. Open Monday through Saturday. Fee. (423) 266-8658 or 757-0020; www.caamhistory.com.

Creative Discovery Museum. 321 Chestnut Street. Kids can tap their talents in the city's $16.5 million children's interactive art and science museum, located just 2 blocks south of the Tennessee Aquarium. Besides having buckets of fun, youngsters can participate in a variety of activities in imaginative settings. An artist's studio, musician's workshop, field scientist's laboratory, inventor's workshop, toddler's play space, performance theater, live demonstrations, and changing exhibitions make this an exceptional attraction for kids. Open daily March through Labor Day; closed Wednesday from September through February. Also closed Thanksgiving Day, Christmas Eve, and Christmas Day. Fee. (423) 756-2738; www.cdmfun.org.

Houston Museum of Decorative Arts. 201 High Street. This grouping of glassware and collectibles has a long and tangled tale behind it. The items belonged to Anna Safley Houston, a local antiques dealer who lived from 1876 to 1951. Married ten times, eccentric, and so poor at one time that she slept in a drafty barn, she was also wedded to her antiques. The museum showcases her extensive collection, which is supposed to be one of the largest in the country. Many of the glass pitchers are hung from the ceiling in the comfortable old house, which is what Houston did when she needed more room for her antiques in her own home. Guided tours conducted daily and there is a shop with unusual gift items. Open Monday through Friday.

Fee. (423) 267-7176; www.chattanooga.net/membersites/houston.

Hunter Museum of American Art. 10 Bluff View. Perched above the Tennessee River, the Hunter Museum houses one of the most important collections of American art in the Southeast. The mansion once belonged to Coca-Cola magnate George Thomas Hunter and now contains the art museum's permanent collection; an attached modern building displays more than thirty touring shows each year. A sculpture garden, lectures, films, and other special programs round out the museum experience. The museum is undergoing a $19.5-million expansion and renovation and will be closed until spring 2005. (423) 267-0968; www.huntermuseum.org.

International Towing and Recovery Hall of Fame & Museum. 3515 Broad Street. This unusual museum exhibits wreckers and towing equipment dating back to 1916, the year the towing industry was born in Chattanooga. Visitors can see a 1926 Ford Model T with a Manley Crane, a 1929 Chrysler with a Weaver three-ton Auto Crane, and a 1974 F-350 Ford with a Vulcan cradle snatcher in the $1.5-million museum. A Hall of Fame honors individuals from around the world who have advanced the industry and includes other memorabilia and artifacts. Open daily. Closed major holidays. Fee. (423) 267-3132; www.internationaltowingmuseum.org.

Maclellan Island. Off Tremont Street. This twenty-acre island in the middle of the Tennessee River is home to a wealth of plants, animals, and birds. A colony of great blue herons resides here, and the island is a feeding area for migrating warblers. The woodland is a Chattanooga Audubon Society Sanctuary and can be reached by ferryboat from Ross's Landing. Ask about the society's other wildlife sanctuaries. Call ahead for hours. Fee. (423) 892-1499; www.audubonchattanooga.org/island.html.

Southern Belle. 201 Riverfront Parkway, Pier 2. For a look at Chattanooga from the water, take a sightseeing cruise on the *Southern Belle* riverboat. As the 500-passenger craft winds its way down the Tennessee River, those aboard hear interesting commentary on the city's history. Lunch and dinner excursions also are offered, featuring live entertainment from country music to gospel. Ask about special holiday cruises and fall color trips. The *Southern Belle* departs from Ross's Landing, near the Tennessee Aquarium. Regular season cruises April through December; weekends in February and March; closed January. Weddings are also conducted on the riverboat, and it is available for other special events. Fee. (800) 766-2784 or (423) 266-4488; www.chattanoogariverboat.com.

Tennessee Riverpark. 4301 Amnicola Highway. Walk, jog, or bike on this developing trail that now stretches along the banks of the Tennessee River (when completed, the trail will extend for 22 miles). The Riverwalk, just one section of the Riverpark, is a continuous circuit of parks, trails, and landmarks that will eventually reach from Chickamauga Dam through downtown Chattanooga to Moccasin Bend National Park. A zigzag path—sometimes called the Wave—from Ross's Landing to the Hunter Museum is a fun way to travel from site to site, and another section continues to the historic homes of Battery Place. Fishing piers, a children's playground, picnic areas, boat launches, a rowing center, floating docks, and a forty-acre public park are also part of the greenway. Open daily. Free. (423) 493-9239; www.hamiltontn.gov/parks/riverpark.

Walnut Street Bridge. Walnut Street. It's hard to miss this bridge—more than one hundred years old—since it now sports a coat of brilliant blue paint. The restored thoroughfare spans the Tennessee River and connects the Ross's Landing/Hunter Museum Riverpark segment with the North Shore shopping and dining district. The bridge—said to be the longest pedestrian walkway bridge in the world—offers a nice way to see the city without the hassle of cars and is open for walking, bicycling, and skating (no skateboards). The Maurice H. Martin Amphitheater is located beneath the bridge. Open daily.

WHERE TO SHOP

Brock Candyland. 200 Market Street. Candyland is only 1 block from the aquarium, so it's hard to make excuses. Select from bulk and boxed candy, lollipops, fresh-squeezed lemonade, soft drinks, and even banana splits from the ice cream shop. Open daily. (423) 267-4496.

Plum Nelly. 1101 Hixson Pike. Plum Nelly began as an outdoor art show back in 1947. Nowadays the shows are no longer held, but the shop carries a large selection of contemporary crafts, with an enormous amount of functional pottery, jewelry, paintings, and sculpture. There is a large selection of wind chimes made of wood, steel, glass, and metal. More than 400 American artists are represented. Open Monday through Saturday. (423) 266-0585.

River City Apparel and Camping Outlet. 14 Frazier Avenue. There's no need to pay full price for an L.L.Bean flannel shirt. Ditto a J. Crew down jacket or an Eddie Bauer sweater. Just drop by this North Chattanooga shop for discounts on items from a wide array of catalog companies. Many items are stock overruns, irregulars, and discontinued merchandise, which are bought from the manufacturers that make them for the name brands. Open daily. (423) 266–4265.

River Gallery. 400 East Second Street. Although the place feels almost like a museum, the handcrafted pieces in the River Gallery are all for sale. Jewelry, sculpture, ceramics, textiles, and paintings are on display here, spotlighting artists from this country and abroad. Around the corner, at 214 Spring Street, you will find the River Gallery Sculpture Garden. Located on a bluff overlooking the river, the garden displays beautiful three-dimensional art pieces, most of which are for sale. The sculpture garden changes exhibits each June. Both the gallery and garden are open daily. (800) 374–2923 or (423) 265–5033, ext. 5; www.river-gallery.com.

Warehouse Row Factory Outlet Shops. 1110 Market Street. People come from miles away just to shop at Warehouse Row, which offers designer brands at substantial savings. Eight historic railway warehouses have been transformed into a comfortable but not overwhelming shopping experience. A few of the forty-odd outlet stores include Tommy Hilfiger, Coach, Bass Co., Polo/Ralph Lauren, Oshkosh, and Nine West. A food court on the lower level is a popular place to stop for a bite to eat. Open daily. (423) 267–1111 or (888) 260–7620.

WHERE TO EAT

Back Inn Cafe. 411 East Second Street. In the back of the Bluff View Inn (see "Where to Stay"), visitors to Chattanooga will find a great place to dine. This bistro specializes in global cuisine with dishes showing both multiethnic and regional influences. Indoor and outdoor seating overlooking the Tennessee River makes this a good choice for a meal, even with children. Open for lunch and dinner daily. $$–$$$. (423) 265–5033, ext. 1.

Big River Grille and Brewing Works. 222 Broad Street. Stop in this former trolley barn to dine on grilled and smoked entrees, pasta, wood-fired pizzas, and creative salads. Toss down one of the several different types of beer made on the premises with your meal or one of the handmade sodas. Rhythm & Brews, featuring live music Wednesday through Saturday nights, is a live music venue adjacent to Big River. There is an access door between the two establishments. A short walk from the aquarium, Big River is open for lunch and dinner daily. $$. (423) 267-2739.

The Loft. 328 Cherokee Boulevard. The Loft has been serving Chattanoogans for years, and you'll have to cross the river to get to it. Steaks, seafood, and prime rib are the house specialties, served in a comfortable dining room with a stone fireplace. Open for lunch Monday through Friday and brunch on Sunday; dinner served daily. $$-$$$. (423) 266-3061.

Mayor's Mansion Inn. 801 Vine Street. The dining room inside this lovely bed-and-breakfast (see "Where to Stay") presents innovative cuisine to both B&B guests and visitors, with a menu that changes seasonally. Entrees such as osso buco with broiled tomatoes and herb polenta, honey-glazed ham with black-eyed peas, and chicken marsala will whet your appetite. A four-course dinner is offered on Friday and Saturday evenings. Reservations required. $$$. (423) 265-5000; www.mayorsmansioninn.com.

Mount Vernon Restaurant. 3509 Broad Street. Conveniently located between Chattanooga and Lookout Mountain, this is a good place to take the family. The salads, sandwiches, fried chicken, spaghetti, and steaks here will please anybody's palate, as will the amaretto creme pie. Mount Vernon has been serving locals since 1955. Open Monday through Friday for lunch and dinner; dinner only on Saturday. $$. (423) 266-6591.

Porter's Steakhouse. 827 Broad Street (in the Sheraton Read House). Porter's Steakhouse brings its Chicago-style fine dining restaurant to the Read House, making it the only Porter's in the Southeast. Steaks, seafood, pasta, ribs, chicken, and chops are the backbone of the large menu, which also includes soups, specialty salads, and a good selection of a la carte items. Open daily for lunch and dinner. $$-$$$. (423) 266-4121; www.porterssteakhouse.com.

Rembrandt's Coffee House. 204 High Street. Rembrandt's is a pleasant place to cap off an evening. Stop by for coffee, pastries, handmade chocolates, deli sandwiches, and soups. The outdoor terrace is a nice place to lounge in the warmer months, and you can get a box lunch to go from Rembrandt's to enjoy in the nearby River Gallery Sculpture Garden (see "Where to Shop"). Open for breakfast, lunch, and dinner daily. $-$$. (423) 265-5033, ext. 3.

Sekisui. 200 Market Street. Located near the Tennessee Aquarium, this restaurant specializes in Japanese food, especially sushi. Give the Tornado Roll a try. Open daily for lunch and dinner. $$. (423) 267-4600; www.sekisuiusa.com/chattanoogadinner.htm.

Tony's Pasta Shop & Trattoria. 212-B High Street. Located in the Bluff View Art District, Tony's serves freshly made pasta—ravioli, tortellini, lasagna, manicotti—as well as salads, calzones, and sandwiches. You can dine outside on wrought-iron tables, head upstairs, or carry out the sauces, salads, pastas, and freshly baked breads. Open daily for lunch and dinner. $$. (423) 265-5033, ext. 6.

212 Market. 212 Market Street. This is a hip spot to eat if you want an elegant evening out. A wide array of interesting dishes—Creole shrimp, rack of lamb, spinach ravioli, and fresh seafood—will please the most discriminating diner. Lunch provides some of the same salads and entrees with the addition of sandwiches. All the restaurant's items are available in a heart-healthy version or with sauces on the side, and there are several nightly specials. 212 Market hosts wine dinners and cooking classes and serves Sunday brunch. Open for lunch and dinner daily. $$-$$$. (423) 265-1212; www.212market.com.

Vine Street Bakery. 1313 Hanover Street (in the North Chattanooga Riverview area). This quaint cottage houses a popular lunch spot where you can either eat indoors or out or choose the take-out option. Try the tomato basil soup or the chive turkey sandwich. Open Monday through Saturday for lunch, but open later in the day during the week for those who want to take something home for dinner. $-$$. (423) 266-8463.

WHERE TO STAY

There are, of course, numerous hotels and motels in every area of Chattanooga. The city's visitor guide lists most of the available accommodations. With the Tennessee Aquarium such a popular tourist destination, it's best to book rooms in advance because hotels in the downtown area fill up quickly.

Bluff View Inn. 412 East Second Street. The Bluff View Inn actually consists of three different historic properties, all available for overnighting. The C. G. Martin House is an exquisite 1927 Colonial Revival mansion, lovingly restored and decorated with fine art and antiques. Its spot high above the Tennessee River provides a lovely setting, and guests are close to the arts district of the city. Three stately rooms all have large private baths. The Maclellan House, at 411 East Second Street, is a striking English Tudor that sits on a bluff overlooking the river and is the place where all guests should check in. Six finely appointed rooms and one penthouse suite are offered, all with private baths. And the T. C. Thompson House, at 212 High Street, has four guest rooms—named for prominent folks in the city's history who made their homes on the bluff—and two suites. A full gourmet breakfast is served in the Maclellan House, with delicious offerings such as stuffed French toast with homemade syrup, cream cheese and salmon omelets, and fresh orange juice. The Renaissance Commons Conference and Banquet Center is located at 402 East Second Street. A continental breakfast at Rembrandt's Coffee House is also offered as a morning option. $$$. (423) 265-5033 or (800) 725-8338.

Chattanooga Choo Choo Holiday Inn. 1400 Market Street. The city's terminal station, built in 1909, is now a thirty-acre complex with 351 guest rooms, forty-five sleeping parlors in authentic railcars, and several restaurants, swimming pools, tennis courts, formal gardens, and shops (many of which sell Glen Miller's version of the "Chattanooga Choo Choo" song). You can even eat "dinner in a diner" and enjoy a fine dining experience in a train's dining car. (Call for reservations.) The miniature train display—said to be one of the world's largest—will delight the kids, and the hotel's Grand Dome lobby is worth seeing. The Choo Choo offers special packages geared for families, some in conjunction with the Tennessee Aquarium. $$-$$$. (800) TRACK29 or (423) 266-5000; www.choochoo.com.

Mayor's Mansion Inn. 801 Vine Street. This European-style hotel in the Fort Wood Historic District was built in 1889 of native mountain stone. Inside guests will find arched doorways, Tiffany glass windows, parquet floors, carved ceilings, and spacious rooms. The home was renovated in 1995 and appointed with original art, antiques, and sumptuous linens. The eleven suites all have private baths, and a three-course gourmet breakfast is served. Common areas include the Music Room, Ladies Withdrawing Room, inviting front porch, and three dining areas. Guests and visitors can enjoy a meal at the inn with advance reservations (see "Where to Eat"). $$$. (423) 265-5000.

Residence Inn by Marriott. 215 Chestnut Street. This Marriott property, which opened in 1996, stays busy due to its convenient location near the Tennessee Aquarium and the IMAX 3-D Theater. The seventy-odd suites all have kitchen facilities and windows that actually open. An indoor swimming pool and breakfast buffet make this hotel even more attractive for families, and appetizers and drinks are offered in the lobby area during weeknights. $$-$$$. (800) 331-3131 or (423) 266-0600.

Sheraton Read House. 827 Broad Street. The Read House has a colorful history, attracting guests to its central downtown location since 1872. Winston Churchill, Tallulah Bankhead, and Al Capone stayed here, as have many other famous people. In 1926 the original structure was replaced by a Georgian-style building of ten stories, but the lavish interior remained the same—terrazzo floors inlaid with marble, black walnut paneling, gilded woodwork, and Waterford chandeliers. The hotel underwent a massive renovation in 1994 and has just completed an $11 million renovation that will give the property 139 full-size suites and 110 oversize guest rooms. The renovation also includes downtown Chattanooga's first Starbucks coffee and the only Porter's Steakhouse in the region (see "Where to Eat"). An indoor pool and exercise facility are also new. Garage parking and in-house shops are some of the additional amenities. $$-$$$. (423) 266-4121.

LOOKOUT MOUNTAIN

Lookout Mountain can be reached from Broad Street in downtown Chattanooga, or you can get back on I-24 and head west for 4 miles. This is the most well known of the three mountains that loom over Chattanooga. The other two—Raccoon Mountain and Signal Mountain—are northwest of the city; Lookout Mountain to the southwest extends into Georgia. The mountain is glorious during autumn, and the winding road up the 2,391-foot climb passes by some beautiful homes. The view from the top is nothing short of spectacular. Besides its well-known Civil War history, Lookout Mountain is said to be the location of the last battle of the Revolutionary War. The National Park Service has marked the spot (off TN-148) with a historical sign. If you are heading up the mountain, make sure you stop in Chattanooga for food, drinks, and fuel. While there is a lot to do on Lookout Mountain, you won't find a lot of places for these services.

WHERE TO GO

The Battles for Chattanooga Museum. 1110 East Brow Road, Lookout Mountain, TN. Civil War buffs will want to stop at this museum to learn more about Chattanooga's role in the war in 1863. A three-dimensional electronic battle map (with 5,000 miniature soldiers, 650 lights, guns that flash, and cannons that puff real smoke) comes to life in a comfy auditorium. And the two rooms full of authentic displays will also interest visitors. The gift shop sells Civil War souvenirs and books. The museum is wheelchair accessible. Open daily. Fee. (423) 821-2812; www.battlesfor chattanooga.com.

Lookout Mountain Incline Railway. 827 East Brow Road, Lookout Mountain, TN. You can start at either the top or the bottom of the Lookout Mountain Incline Railway, built in 1895, and take the mile-long round-trip ride on the mountain. The 72.7 percent grade near the top gives this attraction the distinction of "The World's Steepest Passenger Railway." The cars, weighing twelve tons each, travel at about 6 miles per hour. The upper station features an ice cream parlor, a snack shop, an observation deck, and the incline's machine room, where you can see the giant gears and cables in motion. The railway is a National Historic Site and makes three to four trips an hour. Open daily except Thanksgiving and Christmas. Fee (no checks). (423) 821-4224.

Point Park. 1112 East Brow Road, Lookout Mountain, TN. This spot atop Lookout Mountain was a key area during the Civil War battle for Chattanooga. Now the park is run by the National Park Service and part of Chickamauga and Chattanooga National Military Park. There are several high points to see here, including the striking stone entrance gate constructed in 1905. Visitors can take in a bird's-eye view of Chattanooga from the Ochs Museum and Overlook, reached by descending several tiers of steps. The Cravens House about halfway up the mountain, open Memorial Day through Labor Day, is decorated in period furnishings. Begin at the visitor center across the road from the entrance gate to orient yourself to the park. Here you can also see a large oil painting of the battle done by an eyewitness who was paid $20,000 to record the history-making event. During the summer, park rangers conduct talks, demonstrations, and daily tours. Open daily except Christmas. Fee. (423) 821–7786.

Reflection Riding Arboretum and Botanical Garden. 400 Garden Road, Chattanooga. Reflection Riding is a 300-acre botanical garden and arboretum showing a wide array of trees, wildflowers, and shrubs styled into an English landscape. Twelve miles of trails offer dramatic vistas, or you can drive through the area. The nature center features a 1,200-foot boardwalk overlooking the wetland, a wildlife rehabilitation hospital, interactive games, and children's hands-on exhibits. An educational program with endangered red wolves is presented each afternoon. Open daily except Christmas. Fee. (423) 821–1160; www.chattanooga.net/rriding.

Rock City Gardens. 1400 Patten Road, Lookout Mountain, GA. Anyone who has ever traveled this part of the country has spied the painted barn roofs saying "See Rock City," an advertising stroke of genius for Rock City Gardens' owner Garnet Carter. (He also invented miniature golf.) Carter and his wife, Frieda, developed a large walkthrough garden on their private estate in the late 1920s, and in the middle of the Depression they opened the gardens to the public. Best known for its view of seven states from Lover's Leap, the fourteen-acre "City of Rocks" features fantastic rock formations, incredible scenery, and interesting plant life. Each season brings a different color to the gardens, which contain more than 400 species of wildflowers, plants, and shrubs (don't miss the 3,000 blooming tulips in the spring). The half-mile trail leads visitors through tiny crevices and under huge boulders. Fairyland Caverns, created in 1946, and real-life Mother Goose characters will delight little ones. Walking shoes are a must for the trail, and temperatures are a bit cooler on the mountain than in the city. Benches allow trekkers to stop and rest along the way. Rock City has a restaurant and concessions as well as a couple of gift shops. Open daily except Christmas; closing times vary by season.

Fee. (Combination tickets with other Lookout Mountain attractions are also available.) (706) 820–2531; www.seerockcity.com.

Ruby Falls. 1720 South Scenic Highway, Chattanooga. For more than seventy years, visitors have been coming to see Ruby Falls, a 145-foot waterfall inside Lookout Mountain Caverns (some 1,120 feet below the mountain). Tour guides can point out the unusual calcite formations and convey information about Lookout Mountain Caverns, which stay at a cool sixty degrees. The Fun Forest—a five-level activity area for children—includes modern play equipment as well as a tower for viewing the surrounding Tennessee Valley. Souvenirs and food are available, too. The building is wheelchair accessible, but some passages in the cave are too narrow. Open daily 8:00 A.M. to 8:00 P.M. except Christmas. Fee. (423) 821–2544; www.ruby falls.com.

WHERE TO STAY

Many of the national hotel chains are located in the Lookout Mountain area if you want to headquarter here and then venture down into Chattanooga. Independent accommodations also are available.

Chanticleer Inn Bed and Breakfast. 1300 Mockingbird Lane, Lookout Mountain, GA. If you want to stay on top of the mountain, try one of the quaint rooms here. The fourteen stone buildings hidden among the trees were built in 1929, just down the street from Rock City Gardens. The rooms were renovated in 2002, some have fireplaces, and all have private baths and private entrances. There is also a swimming pool for guests, plus a deluxe continental breakfast is served. $-$$. (706) 820–2015.

FORT OGLETHORPE

To get to Fort Oglethorpe, take I–24 east and exit at 180B or US–27. Follow US–27 south for about 11 miles to reach Chickamauga National Military Park. The park has a Fort Oglethorpe address, and the town of Chickamauga is farther south.

WHERE TO GO

Chickamauga and Chattanooga National Military Park. US-27. A 7-mile auto tour will take you through America's first and largest military park, established in 1890 by President Benjamin Harrison. Here two major battles took place during the Civil War, resulting in more than 34,000 casualties. Some of the war's most remarkable maneuvers and most brilliant fighting were said to have taken place at Chickamauga. Today the park is maintained to resemble as closely as possible its 1863 appearance.

The best place to start your tour is at the visitor center, where exhibits and an audiovisual program give some background on the historic events that took place here. The center also contains the Fuller Collection of American Military Arms, a gathering of more than 350 weapons, many of which are rare. There are more than 8,000 acres in the park, with various monuments, cannons, and historic cabins to see. Ranger-guided tours are offered June through September. The visitor center is open daily except Christmas. Free. (706) 866-9241, ext. 123; www.nps.gov/chch.

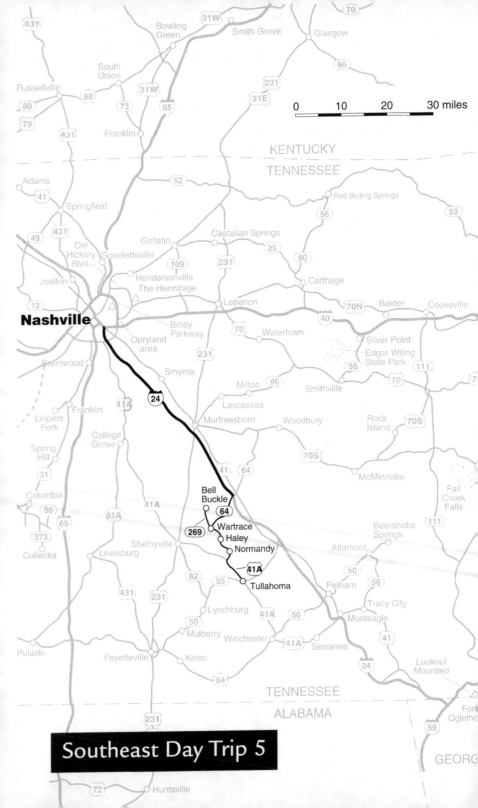

Southeast Day Trip 5

BELL BUCKLE

The best way to reach Bell Buckle is to take either I-24 east to exit 97 or TN-64 west until you reach TN-82. Follow TN-82 for about 7 miles through some beautiful Tennessee farmland, and it will take you right into Bell Buckle. Besides being a recognized community of artisans, the site is known for Webb School, a preparatory academy that has produced ten Rhodes scholars and the governors of three states. You can wander the tree-lined campus and stop at the Junior Room, the original one-room schoolhouse built in 1870. (It's open daily and free.) The school hosts an arts and crafts fair each October that showcases the best in handmade collectibles (see "Festivals and Celebrations").

The heart of Bell Buckle consists of a strip of brightly colored stores specializing in antiques, crafts, books, and art. The quilt painted on the road in front of the strip was done in 1983, when Bell Buckle hosted the National Quilt Convention, drawing some 20,000 visitors to this community of less than 500. Quilt Walk—a quilt exhibition and home tour—is held the third Saturday in September (see "Festivals and Celebrations"). The cafe, located among the stores, has live music on Thursday, Friday, and Saturday night. Stop by on Saturday afternoon to catch the live radio broadcast that takes place there. Most of the retail outlets are open daily.

WHERE TO STAY

Bell Buckle Bed and Breakfast. 17 Webb Road. This Victorian home, owned by the proprietors of Bell Buckle Crafts, is a showplace of what this craft community is all about. Decorated with various handmade items, folk art, and quilts, the three upstairs rooms provide comfortable lodging, and each has a private bath. Enjoy the front porch swing and the homemade breads served with the continental breakfast each morning. $$. (931) 389-9371.

WARTRACE

About 6 miles from Bell Buckle down TN-269 east is the town of Wartrace, where early decisions about developing the Tennessee walking horse were made at the Walking Horse Hotel (see "Where to Stay"). Strolling Jim, the first Tennessee Walking Horse National Celebration winner in 1939, lived in the stables behind the hotel and is buried out under an oak tree.

WHERE TO GO

Gallagher Guitars. 7 Main Street. Country music stars such as Charlie Daniels, Doc Watson, and Grandpa Jones have chosen Gallagher guitars, handcrafted in this small friendly town since 1965. For a peek at the manufacturing process, call ahead and make a reservation for a short tour. Open Monday through Friday. Free. (931) 389-6455; www.gallagherguitar.com.

WHERE TO EAT

Granny Fishes' House. 340 Shipman's Creek Road. This out-of-the-way dining spot is the place to enjoy rainbow trout (raised on the Nut Cave Trout Farm nearby), catfish, shrimp, and frog legs. For dessert, try some of Granny's homemade pies. Open for dinner Thursday through Saturday; lunch on Saturday. $$; credit cards are not accepted, but checks are. (931) 857-4025; www.granny fisheshouse.com.

Strolling Jim Restaurant. 101 Spring Street. Located inside the renovated Walking Horse Hotel (see "Where to Stay"), diners will find Strolling Jim's, named after the famous Tennessee walking horse. The restaurant is known for its upscale Southern cooking, with dishes such as steak, lobster, blackened catfish, prawns, and smoked salmon. Open for breakfast on Saturday and Sunday only; lunch and dinner Tuesday through Sunday in summer, but weekends only in winter. Groups welcome by reservation. A three-entree buffet is offered on Sunday. $-$$$. (931) 389-9955.

WHERE TO STAY

Main Street Inn Bed and Breakfast. P.O. Box 102, 37138. At the Main Street Inn, guests are greeted with refreshments, morning coffee and a newspaper are delivered to your room, and a candlelit gourmet breakfast is served in the dining room. The five guest rooms all include private baths, and some rooms offer step-free access from parking places. Children age twelve and older welcome. No pets and no smoking. $$-$$$; credit cards are not accepted, but checks are. (931) 389-0389; www.historicmainstreetinn.com.

Walking Horse Hotel. 101 Spring Street. Major renovations in 1997 transformed this 1917 railroad hotel. Guests can choose from six deluxe suites, all with private baths and other modern amenities. A banquet room is available for meetings. $$. (931) 389-7050.

HALEY

Continue east down TN–269 for about 3 miles to reach Haley, a tiny town of less than one hundred that draws visitors who want to experience fine dining.

WHERE TO EAT

Our House. 1059 Haley Road (off TN–269 east). This quaint home built in the 1920s is quite a dining experience. Antique tables set with sterling, china, and fresh-cut flowers set the tone for this restaurant, which is remotely sited and hard to find, especially at night. The menu changes weekly, and on a given night it will feature seafood, steak, chicken, or lamb, plus vegetables, homemade bread, and desserts (bring your own wine). The owners claim that some 30,000 people pass through the doors each year. Reservations are required. Open for dinner Tuesday through Saturday. $$–$$$. (931) 389-6616.

NORMANDY

Another mile down the road brings you to Normandy, situated on the Duck River. Normandy Lake is a popular spot for fishing and boating and a picturesque place for a day's retreat.

WHERE TO EAT

Cortner Mill Restaurant. Parish Patch Farm & Inn, 1100 Cortner Road. This inviting eatery, housed in an 1825 gristmill, serves regional cuisine, including dishes such as quail, Cornish hens, and frog legs. Open Tuesday through Saturday for dinner; special holiday buffet meals are also offered. $$–$$$. (931) 857-3018.

WHERE TO STAY

Parish Patch Farm & Inn. 1100 Cortner Road. This working farm is located in the rural hills of Middle Tennessee. The modern inn offers twelve rooms, all with private baths, as well as two cottages. The hosts provide a full country breakfast, and dinner is available with advance notice. The grounds include a pool, an exercise room, and an outdoor play area for children. On a separate part of the farm is the Cortner Mill Restaurant (see "Where to Eat") and four additional guest rooms. The inn also has a conference center. $$–$$$. (931) 857-3017; www.parishpatch.com.

TULLAHOMA

Continue on TN-269 east to the US-41A junction and then head south for about 9 miles. Tullahoma and the surrounding area garnered a place on the map in the early days, when the George Dickel

Distillery opened in 1870. Tullahoma also has played an important role in this country's space program because of the Arnold Engineering Development Center here.

WHERE TO GO

Tullahoma Chamber of Commerce. 135 West Lincoln Street. The friendly folks at the chamber can direct you to various sites in the area. Open Monday through Friday. (931) 455–5497; www.tullahoma.org.

Arnold Engineering Development Center. Exit 117 off I-24, Arnold Air Force Base. This base has been the site of space rocket testing since the 1950s and is presently involved in the development of military jet aircraft, missiles, and space systems. Group tours are available Monday through Friday. Call (931) 454–5655 for reservations; or visit www.arnold.af.mil.

Staggerwing Museum. TN–130 east. This museum contains a collection of Staggerwing and Travel Air aircraft and models, photographs, and documents about aviation's "Golden Age." Of the 800 or so Staggerwings built, only 200 remain. The Beech Model 17 was said to be a milestone in airplane design. Mementos are sold in one of the four buildings that house displays about the Staggerwing. Open daily, but museum is closed December through February. Fee. (931) 455–1974; www.staggerwing.com.

Tullahoma Regional Fine Arts Center. 401 South Jackson Street. Ever-changing exhibits make this a good place to stop if you're in the area. The center is located in a historic building near downtown. Donation requested. Open Monday through Saturday. (931) 455–1234; www.tullahomafinearts.org.

WHERE TO EAT

Emil's. 210 East Lincoln Street. Emil's is a chef-owned and operated restaurant offering fine dining with a French flair in a historic building. Open for lunch Tuesday through Friday; dinner is served Thursday, Friday, and Saturday evenings. Reservations recommended. $$$. (931) 461–7070.

The Stuffed Goose. 115 North Collins Street. Here diners can relax in a tearoom atmosphere while sampling chicken salad, fresh baked breads, homemade soups, and delectable desserts. Open for lunch Monday through Friday. $$. (931) 455–6673.

WHERE TO STAY

Ledford Mill Bed and Breakfast. Shipman's Creek Road. For a bit of solitude outside Tullahoma's city limits, spend the night in a nineteenth-century gristmill. Ledford Mill, which was built in 1884 and restored in 1996, offers three large rooms, two of which have balconies overlooking the woods, creek, and falling waters of Shipman's Creek, and one with a kitchenette, claw-foot tub, and sitting room. Take the stone path along the creek and walk across an arched bridge to the falls. A full breakfast, featuring stone-ground grits, locally made preserves, and baked goods, is included in the price. The gift shop sells an array of items—from antiques and baskets to T-shirts and glassware. $$-$$$. (931) 455-2546; www.bbonline.com/tn/ledfordmill.

College Grove, TN
Shelbyville, TN
Lynchburg, TN

COLLEGE GROVE

The slow scenic drive south on US-31A/41A takes you past small towns and idyllic farmland. The highways split right before you reach College Grove.

WHERE TO STAY

Peacock Hill Country Inn. 6994 Giles Hill Road. You can find peace and quiet and the comforts of home at Peacock Hill, a country inn that's close to both Spring Hill and Franklin. The inn is situated on a 1,000-acre working cattle farm, with stables available for boarding your horses. The pre–Civil War house has five bedrooms, each with a private bath and a whirlpool tub. In addition, the Grainery Suite and a separate two-story log cabin are open for overnight guests as well. The McCall House, with three rooms (each with private bath), is also available and is located just down the road from the farmhouse. All guests enjoy a full country breakfast. Bedtime snacks, fresh flowers, blackout window shades, and music in the rooms are some of the special touches of a stay at Peacock Hill. Dinner is available with prior arrangements, and box lunches can be arranged with forty-eight hours notice. $$–$$$. (615) 368-7727; www.bbonline.com/tn/peacock.

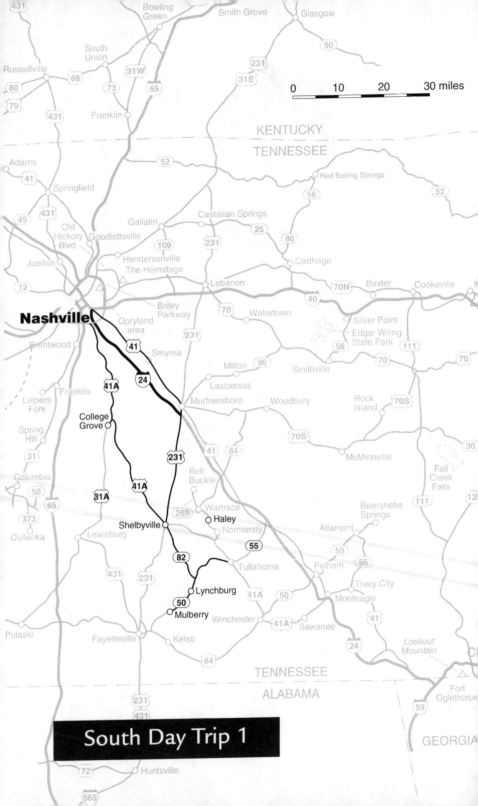

South Day Trip 1

SHELBYVILLE

Continue on US-41A to Shelbyville or head down I-24 to Murfrees-boro and follow US-231 south for about 25 miles. Or if you want to continue on from Tullahoma, take TN-55 west for 12 miles to Lynchburg, then head up to Shelbyville on TN-82.

Shelbyville, a community of some 16,000 residents, has gained international recognition for two things as different as night and day: Tennessee walking horses and pencils. Known as the "Walking Horse Capital of the World" because of the annual celebration in August that draws 250,000 people, the area is teeming with picturesque horse farms and stables (see "Festivals and Celebrations"). It has also been dubbed "Pencil City" due to the large number of pencil manufacturers here.

WHERE TO GO

Shelbyville Bedford County Chamber of Commerce. 100 North Cannon Boulevard. The local chamber can provide visitors with brochures and maps of the area. Open Monday through Friday. (888) 662-2525 or (931) 684-3482; www.shelbyvilletn.com.

Stable tours. There are many places to tour where Tennessee walking horses are bred, trained, and sold. The breed known for its rhythmic, gliding gait was developed in this area in the late nineteenth and early twentieth centuries. A few places to view the "world's greatest show and pleasure horse" include Bridlewood Farm (931-389-9388; www.bridlewood-farm.com), Sand Creek Farm (931-684-0102), and Black Hawk Farm (931-680-1797). Always call ahead, as trainers and horses are often on the road. Some stables may charge a nominal fee. For more information and stable names, contact the Tennessee Walking Horse National Celebration at (931) 684-5915.

Tennessee Walking Horse National Celebration Grounds. Calhoun and Evans Streets. The show grounds, the modern, 2,500-square-foot indoor arena, and the stables are the heart of the area's horse industry and make up one of the largest equestrian facilities in the country. In addition to holding the celebration in August, the grounds host other horse shows and special events. You can wander the grounds at no charge. The museum is open Monday through Friday; Saturday by appointment. Fee. (931) 684–5915; www.twhnc.com.

WHERE TO SHOP

Joe's Liquors and Wines. 633 North Main Street (US–231). For an extensive selection of Tennessee sour mash, including some brands that have been discontinued and are collector's items, stop by Joe's. The store also offers a wide variety of other liquor and wine. Open daily except Sunday and holidays. (931) 684–0777.

WHERE TO EAT

Our House. 1059 Haley Road, Haley. This popular fine-dining establishment is 12 miles from Shelbyville and well worth the trip (see "Where to Eat," SOUTHEAST DAY TRIP 5).

    Pope's Cafe. 120 East Side Square. It's hard to go wrong when the signs shout out TENNESSEE COUNTRY HAM, HOMEMADE PIE, HOT BISCUITS, and GOOD COFFEE. On the square since 1945, Pope's is famous for plate lunches with Southern-style vegetables and homemade pies that will keep you coming back for more. Try the Charlie Pride pie, named after the well-known country singer. Open daily except Sunday for breakfast and lunch. $. (931) 684–7933.

WHERE TO STAY

Cinnamon Ridge Bed and Breakfast. 799 Whitthorne Street. Situated within walking distance of the Tennessee Walking Horse National Celebration Grounds, this lovely colonial home built in the early 1900s has been totally refurbished and offers four guest rooms in the main inn, each with private bath. In addition, there is a separate studio apartment with kitchen off the deck in the back of the residence. A full breakfast is served in the windowed garden room, making for a pleasant place to dine, and there are late-afternoon and evening treats, too. No pets, no small children, and no smoking allowed inside. $$. (931) 685–9200; www.bbonline.com/tn/cinnamon.

Graystone Bed & Breakfast. 300 East Lane Street. Graystone was built in the 1890s and remodeled in 1995 as a B&B in the French country style. Crown moldings, crystal chandeliers, and antique beds have been added to the five guest rooms, all with private baths, phones, and TVs. A full home-style breakfast will get you going in the morning, and the back screened-in porch, where you can admire the lights of the Shelbyville square, is a nice place to end the day. $$. (931) 684-3894.

LYNCHBURG

From Shelbyville, follow the winding secondary highway TN-82 south for 12 miles to Lynchburg. The downtown square has a lot to offer the day traveler, with a quaint array of shops and restaurants. The people are friendly, and the community thrives on tourism. The annual Christmas in Lynchburg event in December is a fun way to kick off the holiday season (see "Festivals and Celebrations"). Lynchburg is the home of the Jack Daniel's Distillery, which is one of the biggest draws for this town of some 350 residents. The town square is the site of the Jack Daniel's World Championship Invitational Barbecue celebration each October (see "Festivals and Celebrations"). Where else can you get a hamburger made with whiskey or a Jack Daniel's sundae?

WHERE TO GO

Lynchburg Welcome Center. Mechanic Street. You will find plenty of information about this small town inside the welcome center. Open Monday through Saturday. (931) 759-4111; www.lynchburgtn.com.

Jack Daniel's Distillery. TN-55. How ironic that the dry county of Moore is home to the oldest licensed distillery in the United States. This distillery, registered with the federal government in 1866, has played a large role in the community over the years and now is the largest employer in Lynchburg. A fun, informative guided tour shows visitors the whole process behind the famous whiskey, including the signature charcoal mellowing used for more than a century. Plus there is free lemonade and coffee in the visitor center at the end of the one-and-a-half-hour tour, where you can also buy (but not drink) commemorative bottles of the historic brew. Visitors can also tour the microbrewery, which is situated inside an old bottling house on the grounds. Jack Daniel's 1866 Classic Amber Lager debuted in 1995 and was an instant hit. All kinds of Jack Daniel's souvenirs can be purchased at the Lynchburg Hardware and General Store in town (see "Where to Shop"). Wear comfortable shoes because the tour involves a lot of walking and climbing. And expect to wait—the distillery is a popular tourist spot, attracting people from all over the country. Open daily except Thanksgiving, Christmas Eve, Christmas Day, New Year's Eve, and New Year's Day. Wheelchair accessible. Free. (931) 759–4221 or (931) 759–6183; www.jackdaniels.com (includes tour information).

Lynchburg Square. This square is where all the action is—a place to wander and shop, and the heartbeat of Moore County. In the warmer months, you can find a farmer selling produce from the back of his truck and watch the whittlers go at their red cedar sticks. Take a break on a bench and soak in the small-town ambience or step inside the courthouse, which was built in 1885. Don't miss the Tennessee Walking Horse Museum on the square. The museum houses exhibits on the history of the walking horse and 150 years of its breeding as well as information on the most recent Grand Champions. (931) 759–5747.

Moore County Jail. Public Square. This jail kept prisoners until 1990 and now is open to visitors who want a look at the cells. The jail is open when a volunteer is available to work. Donations requested. (No phone.)

WHERE TO SHOP

The Lynchburg public square is full of stores for browsing, many selling native Tennessee crafts and products, antiques, and one-of-a-kind gifts.

Lynchburg Hardware and General Store. Public Square. Used whiskey barrels, gifts, cast-iron cookware, country hams, and a plethora of Jack Daniel's souvenirs are found in this old-fashioned store. Open daily. (931) 759–4200; www.jackdaniels.com/general store.asp.

Lynchburg Ladies' Handiwork. Public Square. Old-fashioned sunbonnets, corn-shuck dolls, quilts, and other handiwork line the shelves here. Stop in and watch the women of Lynchburg quilt, crochet, and sew. Open Monday through Saturday. (931) 759–7919.

Pepper Patch Bakery and Candy Kitchen. Public Square. For a sample of the popular Tennessee Tipsy Cake, stop by the Pepper Patch. There's also a slew of other products, including hand-dipped candies, fruit jellies, and various sweet sauces. The open kitchen gives visitors a peek at the candy-making process, and the Pepper Patch will ship their goodies anywhere in the country. (See Franklin listing in SOUTH, DAY TRIP 3, for Pepper Patch's headquarters, which is closer to home.) Open daily. (931) 759–4755.

WHERE TO EAT

Miss Mary Bobo's Boarding House. Main Street (just off the square). Mary Bobo started receiving guests in her boarding house in 1908, serving Jack Daniel and many other VIPs, and the restaurant still dishes out some of the best in Southern cookery. The midday meal served here consists of about ten different dishes—home-grown garden vegetables, meats such as fried chicken and ribs, corn bread or biscuits, iced tea, and delicious homemade desserts. The place seats about sixty-five, and lunch is served family-style. After everyone introduces themselves, a hostess entertains guests with tales of the eatery and keeps the platters moving (pass to your left). People drive for hours to eat here, so reservations are necessary, sometimes even weeks ahead. There is one serving at 1:00 P.M. Monday through Saturday (when the dinner bell rings). However, when enough guests call, Miss Mary's also hosts a sitting at 11:00 A.M. $$; credit cards not accepted. (931) 759–7394; www.jackdaniels.com/tennesseetable /boarding.htm.

Prince's Parlor. Public Square. Prince's makes their own ice cream if you're in the mood for something cold and sweet. There's also pizza and sandwiches, but the real treat is the ice cream. Try a scoop of the Jack Daniel Whiskey Raisin. Open daily. $; credit cards not accepted. (931) 759–4900.

WHERE TO STAY

Dream Fields Country Inn. 9 Back Street (7 miles from Lynchburg), Mulberry. This historic 1860s antebellum farmhouse belonged to Jack Daniel's brother and his descendants for more than one hundred years. It's situated on Mulberry Creek, with 260 acres. Three guest rooms are decorated with country antique furniture, and all have private baths. The innkeepers fill up guests with a country-style breakfast. Bring your hiking shoes—walking trails thread through the farm. $$. (931) 438–8875; www.bbonline.com/tn/dreamfields.

  Goose Branch Farm Bed and Breakfast. Goose Branch Road (3 miles from Lynchburg, off TN–50). This turn-of-the-century farm provides two guest suites, with private entrance and bath, microwave, coffeemaker, small refrigerator, and hospitality basket. A filling continental-plus breakfast is delivered to your door in a bushel basket with treats such as freshly baked muffins, fruit, apple/cinnamon quesadillas, and homemade sourdough bread. Candlelight dinners can be arranged in advance as well. Overnighters are invited to explore the farm or just relax on the front porch. Special-occasion packages are available, too. $$. (931) 759–5919; www.bbonline.com/tn/gbfarmbb.

  Lynchburg Bed and Breakfast. Mechanic Street. Located within walking distance of the distillery and town square, this cute clapboard home built in 1877 offers two rooms with private baths. A continental breakfast is served. $$. (931) 759–7158; www.bbonline.com/tn/lynchburg.

FAYETTEVILLE

For a scenic ride to Fayetteville, go south on US–31A/41A (or Nolensville Road), continuing on US–31A when the highway splits just before College Grove. You pass through the small town of Lewisburg on the way, known for the Tennessee Walking Horse Breeders and Exhibitors Association, where membership services are coordinated (931–359–1574). From Lewisburg, take US–431 south for 25 miles to reach Fayetteville. For a more direct route, take I–65 south to US–64 east, then travel about 20 miles to the town that made the "slawburger" famous. Fayetteville offers the only sanctioned harness racing in the state during the annual Lincoln County Fair in September (see "Festivals and Celebrations"), and gets in the holiday spirit with Fayetteville . . . Host of Christmas Past in November.

WHERE TO GO

Fayetteville–Lincoln County Chamber of Commerce. 208 South Elk Avenue. For more information about the area, stop by the chamber Monday through Friday. (931) 433–1235; www.vallnet .com/chamberofcommerce.

Courthouse Square. The hub of activity in Fayetteville is the square, which visitors will find circled with restaurants and shops. Most any day you will see whittlers sitting on a bench catching up on the day's news and passing the time, which is marked by the chiming of the courthouse bell.

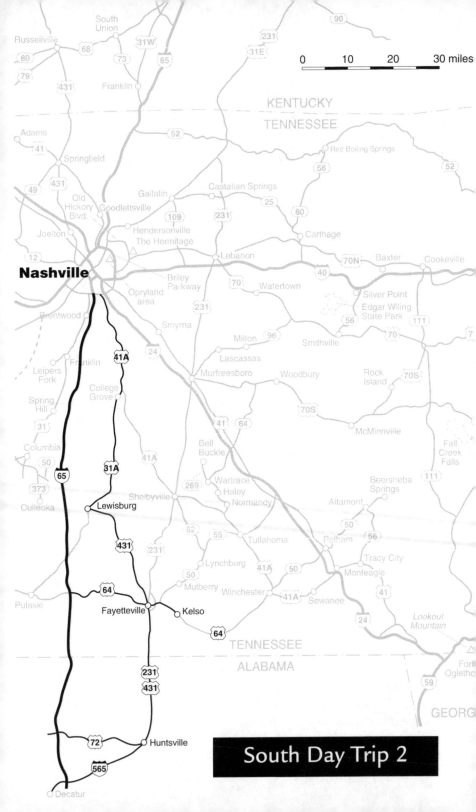

South Day Trip 2

Mockingbird Antique Mall and Ice Cream Parlor. 100 College Street. This is a great place to explore if you're wandering around the square. There's a soda shop and a variety of antiques of all kinds. (931) 438–0058.

Elk River Canoe Rental. US-64 east (9 miles from Fayetteville), Kelso. Canoe the Elk River for a relaxing time outdoors. The river has a good current but no threatening rapids, and the seven different trips can accommodate all types of canoeists. The facilities provide canoes or kayaks, life vests, paddles, and transportation to and from the river. Call for reservations. Open April through October. Fee. (931) 937–6886; www.elkrivercanoes.com.

WHERE TO SHOP

Fayetteville Antique Mall. 112 East College Street. This mall's many booths feature all kinds of collectibles, from starched white linens to glassware and furniture. Open Monday through Saturday. (931) 433–1231.

Marbles Mercantile. 121 Main Street (in the Magnolia Mall). This old-time store sells—you guessed it—marbles of every hue as well as Tennessee salt-glazed stoneware, butter molds, and whirligigs. Open Monday through Saturday. (931) 433–9987.

P. Fitz. 100 East College Street. This inviting gift shop, in one of the oldest buildings in town, is filled with folk art, toys, and a wide variety of gifts. Open Monday through Saturday. (931) 433–8452.

Sir's Fabrics. 110 North Elk Avenue. For more than fifty years, this family-owned business has offered one of the area's largest selections of fabrics, upholstery, notions, and wall coverings. Open Monday through Saturday. (931) 433–2487.

WHERE TO EAT

Bill's Cafe. 111 East Market Street. Bill's serves slawburgers (burgers topped with a sweet-mustard slaw), chili, and stew, as well as other sandwiches. This cafe is a bit livelier than neighboring Honey's, with more locals catching a game of billiards at the restaurant's many tables. Open Monday through Saturday for breakfast, lunch, and dinner. $; credit cards not accepted. (931) 433–5332.

Cahoots. 114 West Market Street. This building served as the firehouse and city jail until the 1970s. The cells' graffiti-covered limestone walls and rope nooses provide nonstop mealtime conversation. The menu features salads, sandwiches, steaks, chicken, pasta, seafood, and a few Mexican entrees. Open for lunch and dinner Monday through Saturday. $-$$. (931) 433-1173.

Honey's Restaurant. 109 East Market Street. Honey's created the original "slawburger," and also gets high marks for homemade chili and beef stew. Old-timers gather at the counter here or go at a game of pool in the back room. Open Monday through Saturday for breakfast, lunch, and dinner. $; credit cards not accepted. (931) 433-1181.

WHERE TO STAY

Old Cowan Plantation Bed and Breakfast. 126 Old Boonshill Road (near the US-64 junction). This 1886 colonial home sits in the rural hills outside Fayetteville, five minutes from the town square. Two rooms, one with a private bath, are offered, along with a deluxe continental breakfast. Tours of the home, grounds, and gift shop are conducted for a nominal fee for groups that want to visit without overnighting. The property is a nice setting for weddings and receptions. $; credit cards not accepted. (931) 433-0225.

HUNTSVILLE

It's a straight shot down US-431 from Fayetteville to Huntsville, and the trip only takes about thirty minutes. If you want to bypass Fayetteville, take I-65 south and get off at either exit 351 for US-72 or exit 340B for I-565. Both highways lead right into the city, but I-565 will take you directly to the U.S. Space and Rocket Center.

Huntsville, originally called Twickenham, was forever changed when 118 German scientists arrived in 1950 to develop rockets at Redstone Arsenal. Since then, NASA and Army engineers have continued to experiment in the space arena. The Army conducts its space and missile defense research development at the Strategic Defense Command in Cummings Research Park. Huntsville's high-tech workforce is the second largest in the nation. The German influence can still be felt, with restaurants specializing in cuisine from that country and a civic center named after scientist Wernher von Braun. For a taste of times past, September brings Old Fashioned Trade Day (see "Festivals and Celebrations") to the square in Huntsville.

WHERE TO GO

Huntsville–Madison County Convention and Visitors Bureau. 500 Church Street. Stop by the tourist office and pick up brochures about the area. Open daily. (800) SPACE4U or (256) 533–5723; www.huntsville.org.

   Early Works Museum Complex. 404 Madison Street. This complex consists of three popular Huntsville attractions—Alabama Constitution Village, Early Works Children's Museum, and Historic Huntsville Depot—plus the Humphreys Rodgers House, which is used for special exhibits and is open by appointment. The complex offers a year-round calendar of activities, as well as overnight adventures and field trips. (800) 678–1819 or (256) 564–8100; www.early works.com.

Alabama Constitution Village. 109 Gates Avenue. Inside the picket fence surrounding Constitution Village, you'll find a living-history museum commemorating the birth of Alabama in 1819. Costumed interpreters show what life was like two centuries ago in nine re-created buildings furnished with antiques. Visitors can see artisans spinning cotton, building furniture, printing, and baking. The Confectionery Shop houses souvenirs and Alabama crafts. Tours are conducted Tuesday through Saturday, March through December; pre-booked groups only in January and February. Fee. (800) 678–1819 or (256) 564–8100; www.earlyworks.com/village.html.

EarlyWorks Children's Museum. 404 Madison Street. Claiming to be "the South's largest hands-on history museum," EarlyWorks Children's Museum features a talking tree, giant-size instruments, a dress-up area with 1800s-era clothing, a 46-foot keelboat, and an interactive architecture exhibit. Kids will have fun learning about early Alabama life with the fascinating exhibits at this museum. Open Tuesday through Saturday. Closed major holidays. Fee. (256) 564–8100; www.earlyworks.com/earlyworks.html.

Historic Huntsville Depot. 320 Church Street. This 1860 depot houses exhibits on transportation, commerce, and industry, with turn-of-the-century steam locomotives and robotic station workers adding to the fun. A permanent Civil War exhibit details the role of the depot in the war. Toy trains, books, and related items await souvenir hunters in the Train & Trolley Shop. A thirty-minute trolley ride through downtown departs from the museum every half hour. Guests can leave and reboard the trolley for no extra charge. Open Monday through Saturday, February through December; call for hours. Fee. (256) 564–8100; www.earlyworks.com/depot.html.

Big Spring International Park. Monroe Street and Williams Avenue. Across from the Von Braun Center in the heart of downtown, this green spot is highlighted by a red Oriental bridge that crosses a lagoon. It's a pleasant place to take a break or have some lunch. It's also home to Panoply, a late April arts event (see "Festivals and Celebrations"). Free. (No phone.)

Burritt on the Mountain. 3101 Burritt Drive. At the summit of Round Top Mountain is a collection of historic structures and a fourteen-room mansion built by a prominent physician in 1936. Living-history interpreters explain what rural life was like in the late 1800s and early 1900s, and visitors can admire original furnishings and prehistoric

Indian artifacts inside the Burritt museum as well as view other rotating exhibits. Wander hiking trails with bountiful wildflowers or attend one of the many special events held throughout the year. The 167-acre park boasts an award-winning Handicap Nature Trail. The park is open daily year-round; the museum and historic structures are open Tuesday through Sunday. Fee. (256) 536-2882; www.burrittmuseum.com.

Huntsville Museum of Art. 300 Church Street South. The nationally accredited art museum's permanent collection highlights American works from the eighteenth through the twentieth centuries, particularly post-1950 graphics. Regional artists and national touring exhibitions are also showcased. The seven galleries are the largest in North Alabama and can accommodate large traveling collections. An expansion in 1998 doubled the exhibition space and increased the art education facilities. Museum-goers can enjoy lunch in the cafe, with a view of Big Spring International Park, and the museum gift store. There's a year-round schedule of events and programs, and the museum hosts meetings, weddings, and other events. Open daily. Closed major holidays. Fee. (256) 535-4350; www.hsv museum.org.

Huntsville–Madison County Botanical Garden. 4747 Bob Wallace Avenue. For a break from the city, stroll the woodland paths of this 112-acre botanical garden and enjoy roses, daylilies, wildflowers, and other blossoms. There is also a fern glade, an aquatic garden, and experimental vegetable and flower gardens. You can lunch in the Garden Cafe and browse the gift shop. Open daily. Fee. (256) 830-4447; www.hsvbg.org.

Monte Sano State Park. 5105 Nolen Road (off US-431). For a beautiful view of the city, head to the top of Monte Sano Mountain, towering 1,000 feet higher than the eastern edge of downtown Huntsville. The park's 2,140 acres harbor a number of scenic overlooks of the surrounding Tennessee Valley. Fourteen rustic cabins decorated with handmade furniture were constructed by members of the Civilian Conservation Corps, the group that developed the park in the mid-1930s. In addition, visitors to this "mountain of health" can enjoy campsites, hiking trails, and several picnic and playground areas. Open daily year-round. Fee. (256) 534-3757; www.dcnr.state.al.us /parks/monte_sano_1a.html.

Twickenham and Old Town Historic Districts. Northeast of Courthouse Square in the downtown area are historic districts definitely worth seeing. Twickenham contains over sixty-five antebellum structures, one of the largest concentrations in the South. Varied architecture styles and beautifully landscaped yards make these homes true standouts. Most were built in the nineteenth century by merchants, bankers, and attorneys; the homes were seized and occupied by Union Army forces during the Civil War. Indirectly this saved them from destruction. The majority of residences in the Old Town District were built between 1870 and 1930, and it is the only predominantly Victorian neighborhood in Huntsville. Pick up a walking tour brochure at Harrison Brothers Hardware (see "Where to Shop") to guide you through these areas. The flyer contains photographs and historical information on fifty-two different structures. In addition, there's a Huntsville Pilgrimage of Homes held each April (see "Festivals and Celebrations"). Free. (800) SPACE4U or (256) 533-5723.

U.S. Space and Rocket Center. 1 Tranquility Base (exit 15 off I-565). This center is the nation's largest space attraction and will wow the entire family with numerous hands-on exhibits, actual spacecraft, and other interesting NASA artifacts. The *Apollo 16* command module that went to the moon is here, as is the original 363-foot Apollo *Saturn V* moon rocket, which was developed in Huntsville. The visitor center explains the history of NASA and houses models of the Hubble telescope and Skylab. Guests can feel the force of 3G's in the Centrifuge or experience 4G's in the Space Shot, a 210-foot tower that instantly speeds to the top at 45 miles per hour. Once there, space fans can experience weightlessness for a couple of minutes. Enjoy an astronaut's view of earth in one of the films shown in the Spacedome Theater or take the Journey to Jupiter, an imaginary trip to the planet in a motion-based simulator. Visitors can land the shuttle by sitting in a simulated cockpit. There are both indoor and outdoor activities, so plan accordingly.

The U.S. Space and Rocket Center also offers a popular space camp, providing intensive astronaut training for youngsters and some shorter sessions for adults. Open daily except Thanksgiving and Christmas; extended summer hours. Group discounts available. Food court and gift shops. Fee. (256) 837-3400; www.ussrc.com or www.spacecamp.com.

Weeden House Museum. 300 Gates Avenue. This residence, located in the Twickenham Historic District, is the only one open as a museum. The home was the birthplace of poet and artist Maria Howard Weeden, and many of the portraits she painted are on display inside. Weeden House offers visitors a wonderful example of Federal architecture, featuring a beautiful leaded-glass window over the front door. Open Monday through Friday; weekends by appointment. Weeden House is also the site for an annual antiques show and sale. Also available for rentals. Fee. (256) 536-7718.

WHERE TO SHOP

Harrison Brothers Hardware. 124 South Side Square. This is Alabama's oldest hardware store and something of a landmark. Founded in 1879, it is now owned and operated by the Historic Huntsville Foundation, which has preserved Harrison Brothers for the public to enjoy. The downtown shop is stocked from floor to ceiling with both old and new tools and housewares, and clerks use tall rolling ladders to get to out-of-reach items. A desk in the store displays a mess of invoices and papers, just as the last Harrison brother left it when he died in 1983. Open Monday through Saturday. Group tours by reservation. (256) 536-3631; www.harrison brothershardware.com.

Huntsville Art League Gallery. 721 Clinton Avenue (in the Market Square Mall). Huntsville's nonprofit art league operates a gallery in the mall with original paintings, sculpture, jewelry, pottery, and other arts and crafts. Open daily. (256) 534-3860.

Lawren's. 809 Madison Street. Lawren's has been a mainstay in Huntsville for fine gifts for years. China, crystal, linens, kitchen equipment, and Godiva chocolates are among the shop's goodies. Open Monday through Saturday. (256) 534-4428.

Signature Gallery. 2364 Whitesburg Drive. Original jewelry, pottery, glass, and wood items by artists from around the country are for sale here. Open Monday through Saturday. (256) 536-1960.

WHERE TO EAT

801 Franklin. 801 Franklin Street. Located in the Medical District, this fine-dining restaurant specializes in continental entrees and offers an extensive wine selection. It has also received Awards of Excellence from *Wine Spectator* magazine each year. Open Monday through Friday for lunch; Monday through Saturday for dinner. $$$. (256) 519-8019; www.801franklin.com.

Gibson's Bar-B-Q. 3319 South Memorial Parkway. Gibson's knows how to do barbecue—it's been the establishment's calling card for more than forty years. Be daring and try the mayonnaise-based white sauce for your barbecue chicken. Top it off with a piece of homemade pie with a mountain of meringue. This Huntsville eatery is also a popular spot for breakfast. Open Monday through Saturday for all three meals; breakfast and lunch on Sunday. $-$$. (256) 881-4851.

Ol' Heidelberg Restaurant. 6125 University Drive. For more than thirty years, the Ol' Heidelberg has been serving tasty German and European food to Huntsville residents. Schnitzel, sausage platters, and specialties such as sauerbraten and beef roulade are served alongside cold cabbage salad, hot sauerkraut, and German bread. Open for lunch and dinner daily. $$. (256) 922-0556.

WHERE TO STAY

There are numerous hotels in Huntsville in every price range. Contact the visitor bureau for a hotel guide: (800) SPACE4U or (256) 533-5723.

The Dickinson. 1100 Locust Avenue Southeast. This circa 1918 bungalow is near the heart of downtown Huntsville. This bed-and-breakfast offers two bedrooms with baths, a continental breakfast, and complimentary snacks. No smoking and no pets. $$. (800) 632-1806 or (256) 539-2164; www.thedickinson.com.

Huntsville Hilton. 401 Williams Avenue. The Hilton is situated downtown across from Big Spring International Park (see "Where to Go") and provides easy access to all area attractions. There are 280 rooms (ten of which are suites), an executive floor, meeting space, restaurant, lounge, pool, and exercise room. $$-$$$. (800) 544-3197 or (256) 345-6565.

Huntsville Marriott. 5 Tranquility Base. After spending time at the U.S. Space and Rocket Center, it's back down to earth at the Marriott, located on the center grounds. There are 290 rooms and suites—some with a view of the Space Shuttle Pathfinder—with complimentary cable television, two restaurants, lounge, indoor and outdoor pools, exercise room, and gift shop. Conference facilities are also available. $$-$$$. (800) 228-9290 or (256) 830-2222.

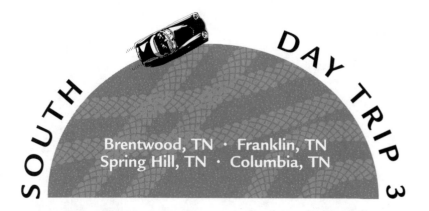

BRENTWOOD

From Nashville, head out on US–31 (Franklin Road) to get to Brentwood, home to a slew of country music stars and a large number of attractive antebellum houses. Brentwood and surrounding Williamson County consistently have the highest per capita income in the state, with a median home price of $338,250. You can take a driving tour to see some of the residences and other structures, most of which are not open to the public. First, get a brochure from the Brentwood Chamber of Commerce at 5211 Maryland Way (615-373-1595) or from the Williamson County–Franklin Chamber of Commerce at 109 Second Avenue South in Franklin's City Hall (615-794-1225). The buildings all have markers in front explaining their historical significance. Tour bus operators take music fans by the homes of some of the stars.

To explore more historic homes, drive along the 90-mile Tennessee Antebellum Trail. There are more historic homes along the trail than in all of Mississippi, Louisiana, and Alabama combined, and they range from town mansions to clapboard-covered log homes. At least ten homes are open daily for public tours, easily recognized by the blue-and-white markers. The majority of homes on the Antebellum Trail are on US–31 south from Brentwood to Columbia.

WHERE TO EAT

City Cafe. 330 Franklin Road. If you have a hankering for home cooking, look no further than City Cafe, where diners can find plate

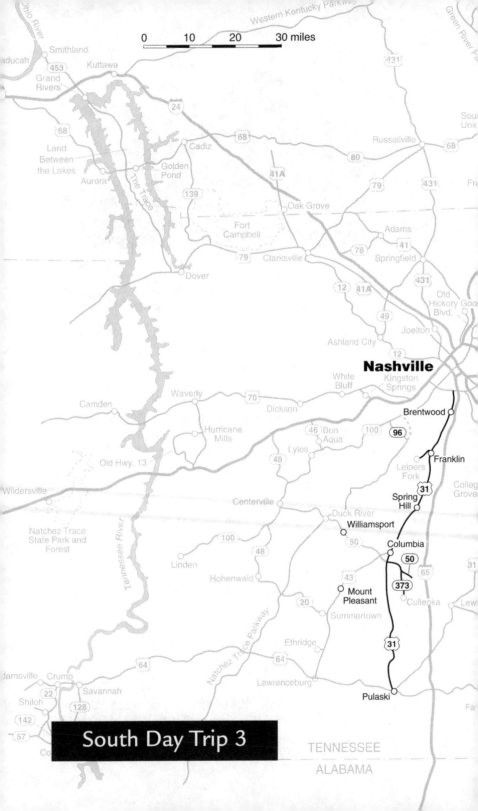

lunches with items such as salmon croquettes, baked ham, pork chops, and a large roster of Southern-style side dishes. Homemade rolls, cobbler, and pie make it seem like you're in grandmother's dining room. Lunch is always busy. Open for lunch Monday through Friday. $–$$; credit cards not accepted. (615) 373-5555.

Corky's Bar-B-Q. 100 Franklin Road. Corky's brings Memphis-style barbecue to Brentwood with both wet and dry ribs, pork shoulder, chicken, spaghetti, hot tamales, and a brisket plate. Traditional side orders accompany meals. A drive-through window makes this eatery hard to pass up. Open daily for lunch and dinner. $$. (615) 373-1020.

Market Wraps. 330 Franklin Road, Suite 908D. Hefty is a good way to describe the creative wraps at this small eatery. All kinds of interesting ingredients are combined inside large flour tortillas and wrapped up for a satisfying meal. Open for lunch and early dinner daily. $. (615) 376-8151.

Mere Bulles Restaurant. 5201 Maryland Way, Maryland Farms, Brentwood. Smart and yet comfortable, Mere Bulles is located in a historic setting—Maryland Manor, originally the main house for Maryland Farms and now an upscale office park. Steaks, chicken, pasta, and seafood are on the menu for lunch and dinner daily. $$$. (615) 467-1945.

Nick of Thyme. 4910 Thoroughbred Lane. This is the place to get goodies to go or relax with a fresh and innovative sandwich, home-made soup, or sweet. Wilma's Whim—oven roasted turkey, avocado, Swiss, sprouts, and honey-Dijon dressing—is a winner, or dig into AK's Kalamata-herbed cream cheese, marinated artichokes, mushrooms, roasted red peppers, Kalamata olives, and sprouts. Salads, entrees, side dishes, and desserts change daily. Open for lunch Monday through Saturday. The restaurant also caters. $–$$. (615) 370-6477.

The Puffy Muffin. 231 Franklin Road. Another local favorite, the Puffy Muffin serves up tasty fare such as crunchy chicken casserole, Caribbean chicken and black bean salad, and simple sandwiches— grilled cheese, tuna, and pimento cheese. Take home some of the eatery's homemade baked goods, or drop by for a slice of cake and some cappuccino. Open for breakfast and lunch Monday through Saturday. $–$$. (615) 373-2741.

Wild Iris Café. 127 Franklin Road. Don't be deceived by the strip-mall location of this locally owned restaurant. You'll find superb

food behind the door. Daily specials, seafood, steaks, and spectacular homemade desserts star on this menu. Open Monday through
Saturday for lunch and dinner. $$$. (615) 370-0871.

WHERE TO STAY

The Brentwood, A Bed & Breakfast. 6304 Murray Lane. Stone
gates on either side of the driveway lead to this Southern-style home,
which claims to be "a traditional bed-and-breakfast with modern
amenities." The six guest rooms include private baths, and a full,
gourmet breakfast starts the day. Several suites with Jacuzzi tubs,
decks, and fireplaces are also available. Afternoon tea and turn-down
service are also included. The Brentwood offers special honeymoon
packages and has facilities for banquets and meetings. $$-$$$. (800)
332-4640 or (615) 373-4627; www.brentwoodbandb.com.

FRANKLIN

Continue on US-31 for about 9 miles and you'll come right into the
pleasant downtown area of Franklin. Founded in 1799, Franklin
prospered as an agricultural center and county seat for many years.
By the time the Civil War rolled around, Williamson County was one
of the richest in the state. The Civil War played an important role
here. Federal troops occupied the area for four years, and one of the
most decisive battles of the war ensued here in 1864, leaving more
than 8,000 dead. Tobacco became the main cash crop after the war,
and the population remained stable for the next century. In the
1960s the area was rediscovered, as Nashville's urban sprawl spread
southward. The completion of I-65 in the 1970s forged the link even
tighter, although Franklin still retains its original small-town charm.

WHERE TO GO

Williamson County-Franklin Chamber of Commerce. City Hall,
109 Second Avenue South. Here you can pick up pertinent informa-
tion about Franklin, recently named one of the best places to retire.
Open Monday through Friday. (615) 794-1225. Brochures are also

available at the visitor center at 209 East Main Street. Open daily. (615) 591-8514; www.williamson-franklinchamber.com.

Main Street. The entire 15-block original downtown area is listed on the National Register of Historic Places. Restaurants, boutiques, and specialty stores operate in renovated nineteenth-century buildings colored blue, gray, and tan. Three annual festivals (in April, August, and December) bring loads of people to Franklin (see "Festivals and Celebrations"). Walking tours are available, with free three-hour parking on Main Street. Contact the tourism offices at (615) 794-1225.

Carnton Plantation and Confederate Cemetery. 1345 Carnton Lane. When this mansion was completed in 1826 (built by a former mayor of Nashville), it was one of the largest estates in Williamson County. Once known for political gatherings and Thoroughbred horses, the plantation served as a hospital following the Battle of Franklin. Guides lead visitors on tours of the home, which has undergone restoration of the rooms, porches, and gardens to make them more like they were during the Civil War. There is a small visitor center and gift shop, and a calendar of special events. The largest privately owned Confederate cemetery in the United States, holding the graves of more than 1,400 soldiers, is at the end of Carnton Lane. Open daily year-round. Fee for house tour; cemetery is free. (615) 794-0903; www.carnton.org.

The Carter House. 1140 Columbia Avenue. This National Historic Landmark was the site of the Battle of Franklin during the Civil War. The 1830 home became a command post, where six Confederate generals lost their lives nearby on the battlefield. The main house still bears bullet holes from the fray. A guided tour of the house and grounds is offered, as well as a museum and video presentation on the Battle of Franklin. The annual Carter House Christmas Candlelight Tour occurs in early December (see "Festivals and Celebrations"). Open daily. Fee. (615) 791-1861; www.carter-house.org.

Franklin Cinema. 419 Main Street. This restored 1936 theater shows art films and popular flicks. You can munch buffalo wings, chips and salsa, pizza, and hot dogs and drink a beer while you watch your favorite movie. Midnight showings are scheduled on the weekends. Open daily. Fee. (615) 790-7122; www.franklincinema.com.

Tinkerbell Park. TN–96 east (Pinkerton Park). Kids can while away the day at this community-built park, which was initiated by the parents of a young Franklin girl who died at age five from kidney disease. It was a labor of love for those who built it, and now youngsters from the area can enjoy forty play stations including the Clown Tube Slide, Spider Web, Space Tunnel, Volcano Maze, and Tinkerbell's Castle. Picnic tables are scattered about, and the Harpeth River borders a large portion of the park. (615) 794–2103.

WHERE TO SHOP

Downtown Franklin is full of shops, carrying everything from antiques to menswear. The following is just a sampling of what you can find.

Bella Linea Fine Linens Downs & Bath. 335 Main Street. *Luxurious* is the only word to describe the comforters, pillows, towels, shams, and accessories found in Bella Linea. The Main Street store specializes in the finest for the bedroom and bath, with a wide assortment from which to choose. Open Monday through Saturday. (615) 627–1884.

Franklin Antique Mall. 251 Second Avenue South. Located in Franklin's historic ice house, this mall houses one hundred dealers in a 12,000-square-foot area. Vintage linens, clothes, old books, quilts, furniture, silver, and cut glass are some of the items in this antiques lover's haven. Pick up a brochure listing other places to shop for antiques, too. Open daily. (615) 790–8593.

The Iron Gate. 338 Main Street. Just a quick pass by the window of The Iron Gate will draw you inside to see the candles, bath products, furniture, bed linens, and antiques. This is a place to find great gift ideas for family and friends, not to mention the irresistible urge to treat yourself. Open Monday through Saturday. (615) 791–7511.

Magic Memories. 345 Main Street. From floor to ceiling this shop is packed with old and new collectibles, many from the Victorian era. Sterling, antique linens, and a large selection of estate jewelry await browsers here. Check out the Civil War memorabilia in the back of the store. Open Tuesday through Saturday. (615) 794–2848.

The Pepper Patch. 1250 Old Hillsboro Road. Tipsy cakes, cocktail jellies, dessert sauces, candies, and butters are this shop's specialties. Gift baskets with all kinds of Pepper Patch goodies can be purchased as well. A branch of the operation is also open in Lynch-burg (see SOUTH, DAY TRIP 1). Open Monday through Friday; Saturday during the Christmas season. (615) 790–1012.

Rebel's Rest. 735 Columbia Avenue. This one-room shop is a Civil War buff's haven. At the museum and relic shop, visitors can see bullets, rifles, sabers, tinware, and paintings among other war memorabilia. Open Monday through Saturday; closed Tuesday morning. (615) 790–7199.

Wessex & Rye. 346 Main Street. Wessex & Rye is yet another of the charming shops on downtown Franklin's Main Street. The store carries an array of home furnishings, garden items, and accent pieces to help make your home a showplace. Open daily. (615) 599–5666.

What's in Store. 407 Main Street. This downtown shop sells handbags, jewelry, shoes, belts, hair accessories, hats, and sunglasses. From ponytail holders to sterling silver earrings, What's in Store can help you accessorize with the latest styles. Open Monday through Saturday. (615) 794–7560.

WHERE TO EAT

The Cool Springs area of Franklin has a multitude of chain restaurants that will satisfy hunger pangs after a day of shopping at the Cool Springs Galleria and neighboring stores. Restaurants such as Tony Roma's, Copeland's of New Orleans, Cozymel's, and Romano's Macaroni Grill all offer great food for moderate prices.

Antonio's Ristorante Italiano. 119 Fifth Avenue North. For a delicious Northern Italian meal, drop by Antonio's to sample entrees such as veal Marsala, eggplant Parmesan, and chicken Romano. The pleasant dining spot is casual but elegant, with white tablecloths and china. Open for lunch Monday through Friday; dinner Monday through Saturday. Reservations suggested. $$–$$$. (615) 790–1733.

Dotson's. 99 East Main Street. You can't beat Dotson's for plate lunches, with six meats and a score of vegetables to choose from every day. Skillet-fried chicken, biscuits, and homemade pies have made this place a mainstay for more than fifty years. Breakfast is served anytime, and there are whole pies to go. Open Tuesday through Sunday. $; credit cards not accepted. (615) 794–2805.

The Franklin Mercantile Co. 100 Fourth Avenue North. This cheerful little restaurant, tucked on a side street near Franklin's

Main Street, is perfect for lunch. In fact, that's all they serve at the friendly Franklin Mercantile. You'll find fresh soups, salads, and sandwiches here on Monday through Saturday, and the place is available for private parties in the evening. $–$$. (615) 790–9730.

Merridee's Bread Basket. 110 Fourth Avenue South. You could hardly find a cozier place to breakfast than Merridee's, with its open kitchen, brick walls, and the smell of freshly baked Viking bread, cinnamon twists, and coffee filling the room. Lunch is equally pleasant, with homemade soups, sandwiches, and salads. Guests can enjoy all kinds of luscious sweets for dessert as well as unbaked pies to take home. The staff puts together gift breadbaskets and will prepare box lunches, too. Open Monday through Saturday for breakfast, lunch, or late afternoon snack. $. (615) 790–3755.

The Stoveworks. 230 Franklin Road. Located inside The Factory at Franklin (a renovated stove factory that's now full of shops), this is a great spot to grab a quick tasty lunch while shopping at The Factory. You'll find Southern specialties such as chicken salad along with fresh soups, salads, and good tea punch. Open Monday through Saturday for lunch. $–$$. (615) 791–6065; www.factoryatfranklin.com.

Uncle Bud's Catfish Restaurant. 1214 Lakeview Drive (and other locations in the surrounding area). Catfish, chicken, and all the fixings—including white beans, fries, hush puppies or biscuits, slaw, pickles, and sweet onions (as much as you want)—are what's in store at Uncle Bud's. Guests so moved also can order frog legs and wild gator tail. As if it needs anything else, this country-style restaurant also claims to have the world's largest ball cap collection. Children six and under eat free. Open for dinner daily; lunch Friday, Saturday, and Sunday. $$. (615) 790–1234.

WHERE TO STAY

Inn at Walking Horse Farm. 1490 Lewisburg Pike (6 miles from Franklin). This forty-acre working horse farm offers four full bedrooms, each with private bath, and a full country breakfast. There's plenty of space to go hiking around the farm, or you can relax at the 10,000-square-foot house and enjoy billiards, the fireplace, one of the three TV areas, or one of the big porches. The inn can also accommodate your horse with advance notice. $$. (615) 790–2076 or

(615) 790–2022; www.bbonline.com/tn/walkinghorse.

Magnolia House Bed & Breakfast. 1317 Columbia Avenue. Located about 2 blocks from the Historic Carter House (see "Where to Go"), this in-town bed-and-breakfast is housed in a completely renovated circa 1905 Craftsman-style brick bungalow. Four guest rooms, all with private baths, are available, and a full Southern breakfast greets guests in the morning. $$. (615) 794–8178; www.bbonline.com/tn/magnolia.

Namaste Acres Country Ranch Inn. 5436 Leipers Creek Road (12 miles southwest of Franklin, near the Natchez Trace Parkway). This bed-and-breakfast gets its name from the traditional Indian greeting, which is known as "an honorable tribute from one being to another." Outdoor enthusiasts will enjoy access to the 24-mile horse and hiking trail, which was part of the original Natchez Trace (see SOUTHWEST, DAY TRIP 1). Ask about the horseback riding package on the Trace. The Dutch Colonial country home has three suites with private baths and private entrances and is accented by Civil War memorabilia, Native American artifacts, and items from the Old West. Queen-size beds, mini-refrigerators, coffeemakers, and televisions add to your comfort. Other amenities include pool, hot tub, fire pit for campfires, and facilities to accommodate horses. $$. (615) 791–0333; www.bbonline.com/tn/namaste.

Windsong Farm. 3373 Sweeney Hollow Road (about 10 miles west of Franklin). If you want to enjoy peace and quiet, reserve one of the two rooms made available at this working farm. You'll find that some of your neighbors are Arabian horses, cows, goats, ducks, and swans. The Japanese room is outfitted with a futon and looks out onto a Japanese garden, while a view of the hills can be taken in from the other guest room. Visitors enjoy a full breakfast, with homemade muffins and jam and freshly made coffee cake to complement the meal. $$; credit cards not accepted. (615) 794–6162.

SPRING HILL

Take US–31 south to get to the small Tennessee town of Spring Hill, which became famous when General Motors landed the Saturn car manufacturing plant here in 1985.

WHERE TO GO

Rippavilla Plantation & Mule Museum. 5700 Main Street. This 1852 plantation home underwent a massive million-dollar restoration after the Saturn Corporation put it in the hands of Maury County. Guided tours explain the historic home's prominent role in the Civil War and the evolution of its ownership. The Mule Museum showcases farming machinery and artifacts from the late nineteenth and early twentieth centuries. The thirty acres surrounding the plantation provide a bucolic setting for Rippavilla, which is the headquarters for the Tennessee Antebellum Trail tour and a regional visitor center. A lovely gift shop carries unusual items. Available for parties, meetings, and weddings. Open Tuesday through Sunday. Fee. (931) 486-9037; www.rippavilla.org.

    Saturn Welcome Center. 100 Saturn Parkway. Saturn car fans can visit the welcome center, a renovated horse barn. Learn about the history of the Saturn Corporation, the manufacturing process, and the car company's efforts to recycle car parts. Visitors will find interactive kiosks, videos, and even information about the history of Haynes Haven Stock Farm, the former home of a two-time Grand Champion Tennessee walking horse. Plant tours to see the cars being built are offered as well but must be scheduled in advance (800-326-3321). Open Monday through Thursday. Free. www.saturn.com (includes information on their annual Tennessee "Homecoming").

WHERE TO SHOP

Early's Honey Stand. US-31. The sign reads THE SOUTH'S MOST FAMOUS OLD-TIME MEATING HOUSE, and Early's has been selling their meats—country ham, bacon, smoked sausage, ribs, and barbecue—since 1925. You can find flour, jam, sauces, cheese, soups, and dips there, too. Pick up a mail-order catalog on the way out. Call ahead for hours. From the day after Thanksgiving to New Year's Eve, the store is open almost daily. Open Wednesday through Saturday. (800) 523-2015 or (931) 302-2230; www.earlysgifts.com.

COLUMBIA

Continue on US-31 for 7 miles to reach Columbia, a town of antebellum homes, one of which belonged to President James K. Polk's family. Mule Day, an April celebration honoring the county's history in mule trading, draws visitors from around the world (see "Festivals and Celebrations").

WHERE TO GO

Maury County Convention and Visitors Bureau/Middle Tennessee Visitors Bureau. 8 Public Square. Here you can collect information about the Columbia area as well as brochures on walking and driving tours. The Visitors Bureau stages tours of antebellum homes in the area, many with Civil War histories. Call for times and fees. The Antebellum Trail Guide can help you find the many historic homes and sites in this area. Open Monday through Friday. (888) 852-1860 or (931) 381-7176.

The Athenaeum. 808 Athenaeum Street. This Gothic and Moorish building, completed in 1837, served as a residence and well-known girls' school until 1903. Maple floors, glass side panels made in Europe, and the original chandelier remain. The structure is now owned and maintained by the Maury County Chapter of the Association for the Preservation of Tennessee Antiquities, and it can be reserved for receptions, weddings, and meetings. A light lunch and tea service are available by reservation from May through December and can be reserved for groups ($-$$; credit cards not accepted). Open for guided tours Tuesday through Saturday, February through December. The home is also on view during the Majestic Middle Tennessee Fall Tour (see "Festivals and Celebrations" under September). Fee. (931) 381-4822 or (931) 540-0741.

Monsanto Ponds. Monsanto Road (off TN-50 west). Bird-watchers and nature lovers will want to flock to Monsanto Ponds, one of the state's premier wildlife observation areas. Monsanto Chemical Company used to maintain a plant here that produced elemental phosphorus. Over the years the tailing ponds used for the settling of solids in the production process offered cover for wildlife and nesting sites. When the manufacturing operation closed in 1986, the company committed itself to keeping the area a sanctuary for birds and animals. The site now spreads across 5,345 acres, 200 of which comprise an observation area open to the public. There are three large blinds for viewing and a visitor center. Open daily from sunrise to sundown. Free. (931) 381–7176.

James K. Polk Home. 301 West Seventh Street. James K. Polk, the eleventh president of the United States, began his political career in his parents' home in Columbia. Now a National Historic Landmark, the 1816 structure is the only existing place other than the White House where Polk lived. Many of the furnishings and personal belongings in the house were used by Polk and his wife, Sarah. Visitors can see an interesting collection of family portraits as well as the former president's inaugural Bible. Next door, a small museum traces the famous Tennessean's life and career. Open daily. Fee. (931) 388–2354; www.jamespolk.com.

The River Rat's Canoe Rental. 4361 Highway 431. Located 5 miles off I–65, at US–431 and US–99. Proprietor Ernie Stewart can outfit you for a day of canoeing on the Duck River, a medium-size river that flows through some of the state's least-populated counties. Canoeists can take in the scenic hollows and bluffs along the river, with forests of oak, hickory, maple, and tulip poplar. Trips vary from a 5-mile, two-hour journey to a 29-mile, overnight excursion. All equipment is furnished, and trips can accommodate both the beginner and experienced paddler. Open seasonally. (931) 381–2278; www.riverratcanoe.com.

WHERE TO SHOP

Accents and Antiques. 3738 Public Square. Twenty-five dealers sell fine antiques and collectibles, including glassware, furniture, linens, and other accessories at this store, which is located on Columbia's picturesque Public Square. Open daily. (931) 380–8975.

Ye Peddler Gift Shoppe. 307 West Eighth Street. This little gift shop is housed in a cute white cottage tucked on a street near Public Square in Columbia. Owned and managed by a mother-daughter duo, it's a popular place for china, crystal, silver, gifts, tabletop items, and all kinds of picture frames. Not surprisingly, a lot of brides come here to register. It's also a great source for printed fabric tote bags and purses by noted fabric designer Vera Bradley. Open Monday through Saturday. (931) 388-8888 or (888) 569-5550.

WHERE TO EAT

Legends Restaurant. 2401 Pulaski Highway. Stop at Legends for a plate lunch or a more encompassing dinner, with specialties such as prime rib, baby back ribs, catfish, seafood, and steaks, made with Johnny's special steak marinade. Meat-and-two plate lunches are offered every day but Saturday, when restaurant-goers can order off the regular menu; dinner is served daily. $-$$. (931) 380-1888.

Ole Lamplighter. 1000 Riverside Drive. This 1840s log cabin perched above the Duck River is an inviting place to dine, especially on the house steaks and seafood. All-you-can-eat items include catfish and peel-and-eat shrimp. Other entrees include snow crab legs and marinated chicken. A large salad bar complements a meal at Ole Lamplighter. There's also a children's menu for those fourteen and under. Open daily for dinner. $$-$$$. (931) 381-3837.

WHERE TO STAY

Academy Place Bed and Breakfast. 301 Goodloe Street, Mount Pleasant. Mount Pleasant is a short drive from Columbia and is a great little town on its own, complete with a public square with interesting historic buildings. This restored Victorian-style older home features three guest suites, afternoon refreshments upon arrival, and a full Southern breakfast in the morning. (931) 379-3198 or (888) 252-1892.

Leatherwood Forge Retreat Center. 242 Dry Prong Road, Williamsport. Leatherwood is located between Columbia and Centerville, near the Natchez Trace Parkway and the Duck River. Set on 122 rolling acres, Leatherwood is both a bed-and-breakfast and corporate retreat center. The cozy lodge sleeps sixteen and offers a great room with comfy chairs, a big stone fireplace, and a great selection of books and magazines to while away the hours. You can also hike, fish, ride horses, or just plant yourself in a rocker on the front porch. Various overnight packages are available, with options for breakfast, lunch, and dinner, plus snacks and beverages. Leatherwood also sponsors a variety of workshops throughout the year. $$$. (866) 583-9231.

Milky Way Farm Corporate Retreat. 520 Milky Way Road (about 20 miles south of Columbia), Pulaski. This historic Tudor mansion has undergone extensive renovation and accommodates overnight guests, business meetings, and corporate retreats. It was built in 1932 by the founder of the Mars Candy Company. At its zenith, the property had 2,800 acres, thirty-eight barns, and even its own railroad and was known as one of the top five farms in the nation. Some sixty houses for the workers were built, many of which still stand. The mansion's dining room boasts the largest privately owned dining table in the state and one of the largest in the country at 12 feet by 28 feet, seating forty. Milky Way Farm—with approximately 25,000 square feet—now has twenty guest rooms, with both private and shared baths. The guest quarters are decorated with antiques and antique reproductions and plush bed linens. A deluxe continental breakfast is included in the price. Fishing, hiking, and bird-watching are easy on the property's 820 acres. House tours are conducted by appointment for a small fee, and luncheons and dinners for groups of twenty-five or more can be arranged by appointment as well. $$-$$$. (931) 363-9769.

Miss Butler's Bed & Breakfast. 429 West Jefferson Street, Pulaski. This 1888 Georgian/Federalist-style home offers five guest rooms honoring historic figures of Giles County. You can choose to stay in the Sam Davis Room, the Count Pulaski Suite, or the Gov. John C. Brown Suite. The home features a library/conference room and a sitting room for relaxing, and a full breakfast includes eggs, breakfast meat, potatoes or grits, and homemade pastries. Miss Butler's is also available for private meetings, luncheons, weddings, or receptions. $$. (931) 424-0014.

Natchez Trace Parkway

NATCHEZ TRACE PARKWAY

The Natchez Trace Parkway, a 450-mile highway through the states of Tennessee, Alabama, and Mississippi, begins in Nashville and ends in Natchez, Mississippi. To get on the trace, take TN-100 west to the Parkway Access Road, near Loveless Motel and Restaurant. The final 5-mile segment, or northern terminus, was opened in June 1996, making a total of 101 miles of parkway in Tennessee alone. The Natchez Trace Parkway Bridge, which stretches over TN-96 in Williamson County, was the first segmented-concrete arch structure built in North America and winner of the prestigious Presidential Award for Design Excellence from the federal government in 1997.

The trace has been a major thoroughfare since the late 1700s. The scenic parkway was first a series of paths that the Indians used and then became a clearly marked trail navigated by early American settlers. By 1810, the Natchez Trace was an important wilderness road, said to be the most heavily traveled in the Old Southwest. One of its earliest travelers was Meriwether Lewis, of Lewis and Clark fame, who died at an inn near Hohenwald. When steamboats became the preferred method of travel in the early 1800s, the trace once again became a quiet, less used pathway. Meriwether Lewis is honored annually with the Meriwether Lewis Arts & Crafts Fair each October (see "Festivals and Celebrations").

Since 1937, the National Park Service has been constructing a

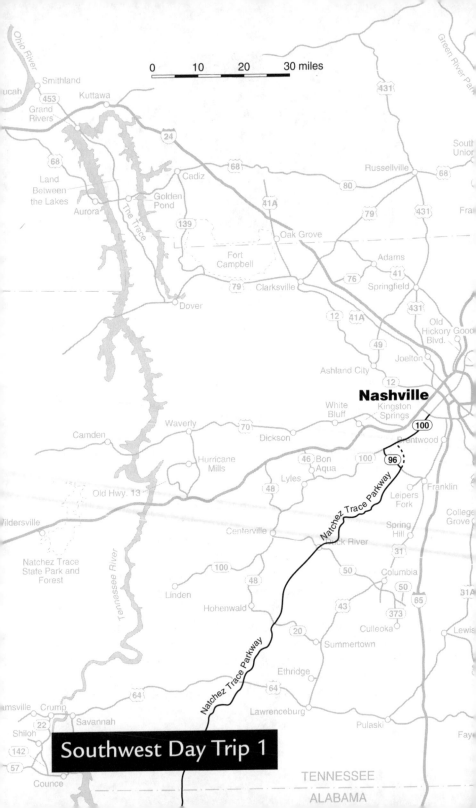

Southwest Day Trip 1

two-lane modern parkway that closely follows the original trace. Now visitors can drive the route at their leisure, stopping to see history and nature exhibits, stands that used to provide shelter for travelers, and historical displays on the Indians and others who used the highway. Mileposts serve as references for points of interest and traveler services along the way. There are lovely places to picnic, camp, and hike on the Natchez Trace. Biking is also popular on the roadway (call for a bicycling information packet to find out about camping sites, sources of water, etc.). A bike route that is part of the Tennessee Department of Transportation's state guides to biking—called "Cycling Tennessee's Highways"—includes a course that takes in part of the parkway as well as nearby highways. Call (615) 253-2422 and ask for a copy of the "Heartland" route.

The pace is slow, with a 50-mile-per-hour speed limit, and commercial vehicles are not permitted. There are no restaurants, gas stations (except one in Mississippi), or lodging on the parkway—just in towns and cities nearby. Deer can sometimes be a driving hazard, and look out for fire ants, snakes, and the ubiquitous poison ivy when walking on the trails.

Numerous bed-and-breakfasts are nestled along the trace, and many are historic homes and inns (see SOUTH, DAY TRIP 3, for a nearby property called Namaste Acres Country Ranch Inn; see SOUTHWEST, DAY TRIP 2, for McEwen Farm Log Cabin Bed and Breakfast). The Natchez Trace Bed and Breakfast Reservation Service (not associated with the parkway) can assist you with accommodations, from moderate to expensive. Call (800) 377-2770 or (615) 285-2777 for information. For a map and information on the Natchez Trace, call (800) 305-7417 or (601) 680-4027; or visit www.nps.gov/natr.

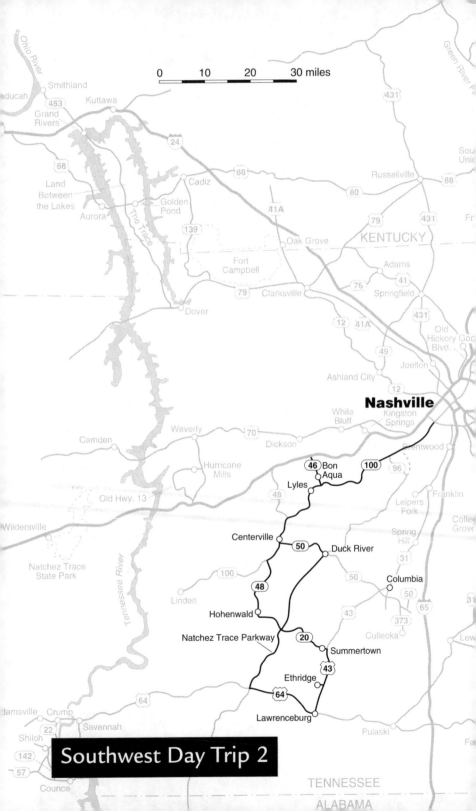

Southwest Day Trip 2

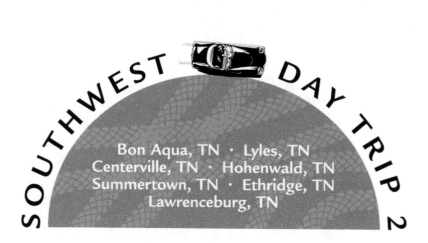

Many of the stops on this day trip are restaurants or inns that are situated in very small towns with nothing else there to speak of. Some of the communities are so close together that you can always drive ahead and then backtrack for food and lodging.

WHERE TO EAT

Loveless Cafe. 8400 TN–100 (18 miles from downtown Nashville), Nashville. This country eatery is famous for its fried chicken, country ham and red-eye gravy, smoked country bacon, hickory-smoked sausage, made-from-scratch biscuits, and blackberry and peach preserves cooked in a pot on the kitchen stove. The restaurant was sold in 2003 and renovated by the new owners, adding more seating and a new kitchen and restrooms. Legions of country music stars have passed through these doors since the place opened in 1951, and some of their autographed pictures line the walls.

Loveless packs them in, so reservations are suggested—and necessary—on weekends. Open daily for breakfast, lunch, and dinner. $–$$. (615) 646-9700.

If you can't bear the thought of breakfast without jam, take a jar home with you as well as the restaurant's mail-order catalog. Gift boxes with preserves, country ham, molasses, and other tasty treats are also available next door at Hams and Jams, where the mail-order company operates, and Loveless caters, too.

BON AQUA

WHERE TO EAT

Beacon Light. TN-100. If you like the food at Loveless, drive down the road a piece for more of the same at Beacon Light. Both restaurants were started by the Loveless family, so it's not surprising to find fried chicken, country ham, biscuits, and homemade blackberry, peach, and strawberry preserves on the menu. Open for dinner Tuesday through Friday, for all three meals Saturday and Sunday. $-$$. (931) 670-3880.

LYLES

WHERE TO STAY AND EAT

Silver Leaf 1815 Country Inn. 7548 Johnny Crow Road. Continue out TN-100, turn left on Johnny Crow Road (right past the BP Gas Station), and then travel on about a quarter mile. The Silver Leaf, a log structure built in 1815, sits behind a large, modern house on a 500-acre farm. This well-known restaurant has been serving guests since 1980 with Southern specialties such as country ham, fried chicken, fresh vegetables, and homemade breads and desserts. Under the direction of Chef Mary Stodola, former director of the Viking Culinary Arts Center in Franklin, the Silver Leaf serves a Southern-style dinner buffet Wednesday through Sunday and is available for meetings and parties. Special menus can be arranged for groups, and feel free to bring your own wine. (There is a corkage fee.) Reservations required. $$. (931) 670-3048.

CENTERVILLE

Centerville, a town of some 1,500 residents, is about 15 miles farther down TN-100 west. This is the place where the late Sara Ophelia Cannon, otherwise known as Minnie Pearl, grew up.

WHERE TO EAT

Breece's Cafe. 111 South Public Square. Breece's has a long history in town, starting as a pie wagon in 1939. Diners will find Southern fried chicken, fresh green beans, corn, squash, fried apples, home-made rolls, corn bread, and made-from-scratch desserts at this eatery on the square. Open for all three meals daily. $–$$. (931) 729–3481.

WHERE TO STAY

McEwen Farm Log Cabin Bed and Breakfast. 1910 Bratton Lane (halfway between Centerville and Columbia), Duck River. Located just 2 miles off the Natchez Trace Parkway (see SOUTHWEST, DAY TRIP 1), McEwen Farm offers a fully furnished log cabin built from the original structures on the farm that date back to 1820. Center-ville's original train depot has been moved onto the property and re-stored as guest quarters, too. The Duck River is within a mile of the B&B, so opportunities for fishing and canoeing abound. A hunting-dog training facility is also located on the property. A continental breakfast is offered, or you may prefer to use the kitchen facilities in the cabin and depot. $$; credit cards are not accepted, but personal checks are. (931) 583–0714.

HOHENWALD

Continue down TN–100, then take TN–48 south. Hohenwald is about 20 miles from Centerville.

WHERE TO GO

Lewis County Chamber of Commerce. 112 East Main Street. Stop by the restored Hohenwald Depot for more information on the area. Open Monday through Friday. (931) 796–4084; www.visitlewis.com.

WHERE TO SHOP

If you like saving money on clothes and don't mind spending the time looking, head to Hohenwald. Known for its "junk stores," this small town is one of the few places you can do bargain shopping for the whole family. A handful of junk stores operate among a downtown of mom-and-pop shops and restaurants. Thousand-pound bales of clothing are shipped in from the north twice a week, and you can spend hours sifting through the piles of used clothing. The retail outlets divide the merchandise into "men's shirts," "babies' clothing," "coats," and so on. You can find old-timey clothes as well as major labels, and the majority of them are in good condition. Prices are cheap—it's easy to walk away with a couple of grocery bags bulging with clothes for $15. Most of the secondhand shops are open daily.

SUMMERTOWN

From Hohenwald, take TN–20 east to Summertown. In its heyday in the early 1900s, Summertown was a popular place to stay during the warmer months and was known for its freestone spring where visitors drank the healthful water. Today, the community is home to fewer than 1,000 people. The Summertown Bluegrass Reunion brings pickers together twice during the summer, entertaining more than 3,000 fans (see "Festivals and Celebrations" under June).

If you'd rather bypass Summertown, you can head back on the Natchez Trace Parkway, which can be reached on TN–20, about 7 miles past Hohenwald. The parkway, once an Indian path and wilderness trail, is now a scenic highway managed by the National Park System that runs from Nashville to Natchez, Mississippi (see SOUTHWEST, DAY TRIP 1).

WHERE TO GO

The Farm. 100 Farm Road. Turn off TN–20 onto Drakes Lane, go about 1 mile, and then veer to the right on Farm Road. The Farm's gate and visitor center lies just ahead.

In 1971, university professor Stephen Gaskin and a caravan of 300 hippies from California headed to Middle Tennessee to create a new social order. The group purchased 1,750 acres and threw all their belongings into a collective pot. Some thirty-plus years later, the communal economy has changed, but the ideals remain the same. The residents run several different businesses here, including a "soy dairy" that provides tofu to both health food and major grocery stores, a book publishing company, a mushroom-growing operation, and a company called SE International, which produces hand-held radiation detectors.

The Farm School operates on the grounds, and Ina Mae Gaskin runs a Farm Midwifery Center that caters to those seeking an alternative birth experience. Visitors are welcome to The Farm, but it's best to make arrangements ahead of time. There is a primitive campground, dorm space at the Community Center, and lodging in some private homes. The Ecovillage Training Center offers dorm-style rooms and private rooms. The Farm Store has various food and supplies. The Farm Experience Weekend is a chance to experience communal living firsthand, with a tour, community dinner, workshops, and entertainment. Retreat and conference services are also offered, as well as lectures and workshops. (931) 964–3574; www.thefarmcommunity.com.

ETHRIDGE

Continue about 5 miles east on TN–20, and then pick up US–43 to get to the tiny community of Ethridge.

Tennessee's largest Amish settlement is here, and members make their living as farmers and craftspeople. The Amish came to the area in 1944 and still devoutly follow the teachings of their religion. No mechanized farm equipment is used, there is no electricity, and the people drive in horse and buggy. Wagon tours of the area provide opportunities for purchasing Amish products. No picture taking is allowed, as it infringes on the inhabitants' rights and beliefs.

WHERE TO GO

Granny's Network. 44 Marcella Falls Road (off US–43); call for directions. For more than twenty years, Sarah Evetts has been operating a ten-watt station from her home in the country outside Ethridge. Granny, who is also the mother of seven children, films whatever is interesting to local folks, and she has been interviewed on the *Today* show and *The Tonight Show*. Visitors can stop by and make a tape with Granny to take home. Open daily. Free. Evetts operates Granny's Welcome Center—on US-43—which is an antiques store/flea market that also sells handmade goods from the nearby Amish community. A horse-drawn wagon tour of the area also begins here. (931) 829-2433.

WHERE TO SHOP

More than 200 families of Amish farmers and craftspeople live in the Ethridge area. You might find residents selling homemade bread, vegetables, baskets, quilts, furniture, and sorghum molasses.

Amish Country Galleries. 3931 US-43 north. Locally handcrafted Amish items such as baskets, furniture, and antiques can be found here as well as crafts by other area residents. The shop's art gallery displays local artwork. Open Monday through Saturday. (931) 829-2126.

LAWRENCEBURG

Lawrenceburg is a few miles farther down US-43.

Although Lawrenceburg, the county seat, was named for a naval hero in the War of 1812, it is frontiersman and Alamo hero David Crockett who is most closely identified with the city. Crockett helped organize Lawrence County in 1817 soon after the Chickasaw Indians gave up control to the United States. A life-size bronze statue of Crockett with rifle and hat in hand was erected on the public square in 1922 to honor him.

WHERE TO GO

Lawrence County Chamber of Commerce. 1609 North Locust Avenue. Stop for information and brochures on area attractions in the chamber's restored log cabin. Open Monday through Friday. (931) 762-4911; www.lawrenceburg.com/chamber.

David Crockett State Park. US-64 (about $1/2$ mile west of Lawrenceburg). This 1,100-acre park honors one of Tennessee's most famous sons. There are two campgrounds, an Olympic-size swimming pool, boating and fishing on forty-acre Lindsey Lake, bicycle trails, tennis courts, and various planned activities here through the summer months. Hungry guests can relax in the large pleasant restaurant that overlooks the lake ($$). The park also operates the Crockett Museum, which depicts the frontiersman's life. Milling demonstrations take place during the summer. Kids begging for coonskin caps and other souvenirs will find them here. Free. (931) 762-9408; www.state.tn.us/environment/parks/parks/DavidCrockettSP.

David Crockett Cabin and Museum. South Military Avenue. This replica of Crockett's office contains pictures, articles, clothing, and other items of the period. Open mornings, but it's best to call ahead. Free. (931) 762-4231.

Mexican Monument. Public Square. This monument, erected in 1849 to honor those who fought in the Mexican-American War, is one of only two in the United States. Free. (No phone.)

WHERE TO EAT

Big John's Barbecue. 904 North Military Avenue. Big John's will satisfy your hankering for barbecue ribs and chicken, self-serve style. It's been a favorite in Lawrenceburg for more than twenty-five years. Try the curly fries and vinegar-based coleslaw, and snatch up some of Big John's bottled sauce to use on your table at home. Open Monday through Saturday for lunch and dinner. $; credit cards not accepted. (931) 762-9596.

Brass Lantern. 2290 Pulaski Highway (US-64 east). For more than a decade, The Brass Lantern has been attracting folks because of its steaks, pasta, catfish, sandwiches, salad bar, and pizza. The King's Crown sandwich—which pairs roast beef, ham, jack and cheddar cheeses, lettuce, and mayo on Hawaiian bread—is a popular choice, as is the prime rib and lobster tail. Take home some of owner Johnny Fleeman's gourmet sauces and dressings. Open for lunch and dinner daily. $-$$. (931) 762-0474.

WHERE TO STAY

The Granville House Bed and Breakfast. 229 Pulaski Street. Located just east of the town square, Granville House was completely restored in 1988 and has five large rooms, three with private baths. Some guest quarters have working fireplaces, and others have private balconies. The 115-year-old antebellum bed-and-breakfast serves a continental breakfast. $$. (931) 762–3129.

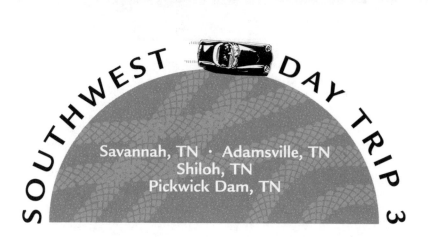

Savannah, TN · Adamsville, TN
Shiloh, TN
Pickwick Dam, TN

SAVANNAH

To reach Savannah from the Natchez Trace Parkway, head west on US-64 for approximately 45 miles. Life revolves around the Tennessee River here, where transportation of goods has been part of the community since it was settled in the 1820s. One of the city's famous residents was Queen Haley, grandmother of author Alex Haley (well known for his book *Roots*). Queen lived in Savannah from the time she was a young woman until her death in the early 1930s. Her grave is in the Savannah Cemetery. July brings the annual Savannah Bluegrass Festival (see "Festivals and Celebrations").

WHERE TO GO

Hardin County Convention and Visitors Bureau. 507 Main Street. The tourism office, located inside the Tennessee River Museum, is open daily for brochures and information on the area. (800) 552-FUNN or (731) 925-2364; www.tourhardincounty.org.

Savannah Historic District. Downtown area. This district consists of approximately twenty historically significant buildings, dating from 1869 to 1930. The Cherry Mansion, said to be one of the oldest structures in Savannah, served as headquarters for General Ulysses S. Grant during the Civil War. Although now a private home, it serves as a backdrop for outdoor concerts by the Memphis Symphony Orchestra each September. There is a 2-mile route through

the district that is ideal for driving, walking, or bicycling. Stop by the Tennessee River Museum or call the Hardin County Convention and Visitors Bureau for a brochure. (800) 552-FUNN or (731) 925-2364.

Tennessee River Museum. 507 Main Street. This Savannah attraction is a monument to the river and the influence it has had on the people here. There are five major exhibit areas and a gift shop. Visitors can see a collection of Indian artifacts, Civil War relics, paleontology finds, and Hardin County history exhibits. Open daily. Fee (free admission with Shiloh National Military Park ticket). (800) 552-FUNN or (731) 925-2364.

WHERE TO EAT

Christie's. 1012 Pickwick Road. Those with large appetites can get their fill here with a country-style breakfast, buffet lunch, sandwiches, and homemade desserts. Christie's has a large banquet room and welcomes tour buses. Open daily for all three meals. $-$$. (731) 925-9285.

Savannah Cooks. 804 Main Street. This favorite local lunch spot offers breakfast and lunch, including soups, salads, and sandwiches, and even makes its own bread. Open Monday through Friday for breakfast and lunch; Friday and Saturday for dinner only. $-$$. (731) 925-8046.

The Wharf. 120 Wharf Lane (off TN-128). "Best fish in a dam site" is the motto here, where the catfish, hush puppies, and slaw are plentiful. The restaurant—which has been a mainstay for more than twenty-five years—also serves up fried shrimp, fried oysters, country ham, and hamburgers. Open for lunch and dinner, Friday through Sunday. Call for winter hours. Group facilities available. $$. (731) 925-9469.

ADAMSVILLE

From Savannah, take US-64 west for 8 miles until you reach Adamsville. On the way you'll pass through the small community of Crump, which stages a popular flea market each weekend.

WHERE TO GO AND EAT

Buford Pusser Home and Museum. 342 Pusser Street. This is where legendary lawman Buford Pusser lived, worked, and eventually died. Those who saw the movie *Walking Tall* and its sequels know his story as sheriff of McNairy County. This was a man who had his jaw shot off, saw his wife killed by assailants, and died in a fiery car crash in 1974. Pusser's modest home is filled with original furnishings and items chronicling his life. The graves of both Pusser and his wife are in the town cemetery. Pusser's restaurant, owned by Pusser's daughter, serves lunch and dinner. Open daily year-round. Fee. (731) 632-4080; www.sheriffbufordpusser.com.

SHILOH

From Adamsville, you will need to backtrack on US-64 to Crump, then catch TN-22 south to Shiloh.

WHERE TO GO

Shiloh National Military Park. TN-22 south. Civil War buffs will be interested in taking the 9½-mile auto tour of this park, which was the scene of one of the bloodiest battles of the Civil War. More than 23,000 men were casualties of the fighting, and 3,854 grave sites are there. The 3,960-acre park, managed by the National Park Service, commemorates the battle with 156 monuments and more than 475 iron tablets containing historical information and notations of camp and troop positions. A short film runs throughout the day, describing the all-important battle, and visitors can browse through the displays about military equipment and the soldiers who fought there. Various programs are held on weekends, including an annual living-history demonstration that is scheduled in early April to coincide with the anniversary of the battle. Call ahead to find out what other events are scheduled. Fee. (731) 689-5696; www.nps.gov/shil.

Shiloh's Civil War Relics. TN-22 south. Located just north of Shiloh National Military Park, this museum/shop carries a large selection of genuine Civil War relics and souvenirs. Nominal admission fee is refundable with a purchase. Open daily except Tuesday. (731) 689–4114; www.shilohrelics.com.

WHERE TO EAT

Hagy's Catfish Hotel. 1140 Hagy Lane (just off TN–22). You can dine on whole fried catfish while gazing at the place these creatures make their home—the Tennessee River. (Hagy's are actually farm-raised.) Lemon-pepper and Cajun-spiced catfish are also available as well as items such as ribs, steak, and chicken at Hagy's, which isn't and never was a hotel. This family-style eatery was named one of the top ten catfish restaurants in the country by the Catfish Institute in 1997. Open Tuesday through Sunday for lunch and dinner. $$. (731) 689–3327.

PICKWICK DAM

Pickwick Dam is about 2 miles farther down TN–57.

WHERE TO GO

Pickwick Landing Dam. TN–128. Construction of the Tennessee Valley Authority dam began in 1934, and the 53-mile-long lake began to fill four years later. The dam is 113 feet high and more than 7,000 feet long. Pickwick Dam is important for both flood control and hydroelectric power, and it provides an important waterway for towboats and barges to travel on. Visitors can watch boats lock through the dam, and there is also a self-touring museum about the river. More than sixty-six campsites are available on a first-come, first-served basis. Open daily except some major holidays. Free, but fees apply for campers. (901) 925–4346.

Pickwick Landing State Resort Park. TN–57 south and TN–128. This state park on the shores of Pickwick Lake is a favorite fishing spot for outdoorsmen. Other water-related activities such as boating, swimming, and water skiing are popular on the lake. Facilities include a full-service marina, an eighteen-hole golf course, campsites, picnic areas, deluxe cabins, and an inn and restaurant (see "Where to Stay"). Open daily, but closed mid-December through

early January. (731) 689–3129; www.state.tn.us/environment/parks
/parks/PickwickLanding.

WHERE TO EAT

Jon's Pier at Pickwick. 11805 TN–57, Counce. This well-known
local spot, which is not actually on a pier, serves more than seafood.
You'll also find prime rib and other specialties. Located about 3
miles south of Pickwick Dam, Jon's Pier has hours that change seasonally, so call ahead. (731) 689–3575.

WHERE TO STAY AND EAT

Historic Botel. TN–128 and Botel Road (just northwest of Pickwick
Dam), Savannah. This retired engineer's quarterboat has been remodeled into a riverside resort that offers a unique dining and sightseeing experience. A large fishing area is equipped with a boat dock,
launching ramp, and playground. The restaurant serves lunch Saturday and Sunday and dinner Thursday through Sunday, with the
specialty being, of course, catfish. But diners can also find country
ham, fried chicken, steak, and sandwiches, and the cook will even
cook your catch for you ($–$$). Six rooms accommodate
overnighters. Historic Botel is open Thursday through Sunday. $.
(731) 925–4787.

   Pickwick Landing State Resort Park Inn. TN–57. A view of the
scenic Pickwick Lake sets this modern inn apart from the others,
with 119 rooms and five suites, tennis courts, a swimming pool, a
playground, and a gift shop. A large paneled dining room with ex-
posed trusses serves Southern-style food to guests. Open daily except
for two weeks at Christmastime. $$. (731) 689–3135 or (800)
250–8615.

KINGSTON SPRINGS

Kingston Springs is only about 15 miles west from the Bellevue Center mall on US–70.

The Harpeth Scenic River and Narrows Historic Area is worth a visit. A 100-yard tunnel, which was hand-cut by slaves who used drills and black powder to get through the solid rock, was declared one of the great engineering feats of the time. Today it is an industrial landmark on the National Register of Historic Places and a subsidiary of Montgomery Bell State Park (www.state.tn.us/environment/parks /parks/MontgomeryBell), just one of Tennessee's fifty-four state parks. (615) 797–9052.

WHERE TO GO

Tip-A-Canoe. 1279 US–70. If you want to get out on the Harpeth River, Tip-A-Canoe, one of the oldest canoe outfitters in the nation, can help you get going. The canoe outpost can help with a variety of trips, from two-hour to four-day excursions on the Harpeth River, which is one of the most historic and scenic waterways in Middle Tennessee. A shuttle ride to the put-in points, paddles, life jackets, and the canoes, of course, all are available here. Group and weekend rates are offered, and reservations are recommended. (615) 646–7124 or (800) 550–5810; www.tip-a-canoe.com.

West Day Trip 1

WHITE BLUFF

Just a short drive down US-70 takes you to White Bluff, a town where the living is easy and the barbecue isn't greasy.

WHERE TO EAT

Carl's Perfect Pig. 4991 US-70. Carl's is known nationwide for its delectable ribs, whole smoked chickens, and classic pulled pork barbecue (get it on corn cakes). Barbecue brisket, catfish, hush puppies, real mashed potatoes, and other vegetables also make the down-home eatery worth the drive. Carl's is open Wednesday through Saturday for lunch and dinner; lunch only on Sunday. $-$$; credit cards not accepted. (615) 797-4020.

WAVERLY

Continue on US-70 through Dickson to get to Waverly, a small town of about 4,000 people.

WHERE TO STAY

The Nolan House. 375 TN-13 north (just off US-70). This 1870 historic home, which is on the National Register of Historic Places, is named after James Nicholas Nolan, a successful businessman who made Waverly his home. Three antiques-filled guest rooms are available, all with private baths. Guests use the television and phone in the common room. The adjoining Great Room (22 feet by 28 feet) overlooks the gazebo. Homemade treats and beverages are served after checking in, and a continental breakfast is on tap in the morning. Try your hand at horseshoes or croquet, or unwind in one of the wicker rockers on the front porch. Nolan House can accommodate meetings and special occasions. $$; credit cards not accepted. (931) 296-2511; www.bbonline.com/tn/nolanhouse.

CAMDEN

Continue on US–70 until you reach Camden, which draws visitors to see a working freshwater pearl farm.

WHERE TO GO

Tennessee River Freshwater Pearl Farm, Jewelry Showroom & Museum. 255 Marina Road. Birdsong Resort, Marina and Lakeside RV Campground in rural Camden is where the precarious process of culturing pearls in Tennessee takes place. "A Pearl of a Tour" takes visitors on a three- to five-hour guided tour in shaded pontoon boats to see where freshwater mussels are raised to make cultured pearls. Guests can talk to one of the divers who harvest mussel shells along Birdsong Creek, which is part of Kentucky Lake. A catered lunch is included in the tour, which requires a minimum group size of fifteen. An optional add-on to the tour includes continuing on to the Tennessee River Folklife Museum in the Nathan Bedford Forrest State Resort area in nearby Eva. The Pearl Jewelry Showroom displays a variety of freshwater pearl jewelry and is open year-round. Tours can be arranged April through October by reservation. Fee. (800) 225–7469 or (731) 584–7880; www.tennesseeriverpearls.com; www.birdsongresort.com.

WEST

DAY TRIP 2

Hurricane Mills, TN
Natchez Trace State Park
(Wildersville, TN)

HURRICANE MILLS

Head west on US–70 and then go south on TN–13 to get to Hurricane Mills. It's also easily reached by taking I–40 west to exit 143, then hopping on TN–13 north for about 8 miles.

WHERE TO GO

Loretta Lynn's Ranch. TN–13. As country music goes, Loretta Lynn ranks up there as an all-time favorite. Her rags-to-riches story came to life in the movie *Coal Miner's Daughter,* and she is one of the industry's most-awarded female vocalists. The country artist now makes her home in Hurricane Mills (she owns the town) and has created a campground and Western town on her 6,500-acre ranch.

Visitors can tour Lynn's fourteen-room antebellum home; her personal museum and gift shop, which has recently been enlarged; the Butcher Holler Home Place, a re-creation of the cabin where the singer grew up; and a simulated coal mine. The refurbished bus from *Coal Miner's Daughter* can also be toured. Campground facilities feature a swimming pool, miniature golf, cabins, and a playground, and special events such as horseback trail rides and the National Motorcross Championship are staged here throughout the year. Lynn is even around occasionally to sign autographs and do concerts for her fans. Saturday night hoedowns take place during the summer, and during the Christmas season, Lynn's mansion is decked out and

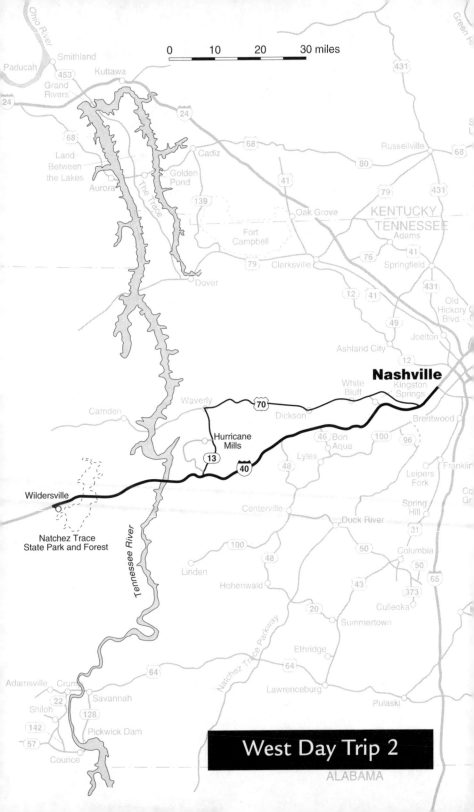

0   10   20   30 miles

Ohio River

Paducah
Smithland
453
Kuttawa
Grand Rivers
24

68

Land Between the Lakes

Aurora

The Trace

Golden Pond

139

Cadiz

24

68

41

79

431

431

Oak Grove

KENTUCKY
TENNESSEE
Adams

41

Russellville

80

Fort Campbell

79

Clarksville

76

Springfield

431

Dover

12   41

Camden

Waverly

70

Dickson

White Bluff

Kingston Springs

Nashville

12

Ashland City

49

Joelton

Old Hickory Blvd.

Brentwood

Hurricane Mills

13

40

48

Lyles

46   Bon Aqua

100

96

Wildersville

Natchez Trace State Park and Forest

Tennessee River

Centerville

100

48

Linden

Hohenwald

Duck River

50

43

Leipers Fork

Spring Hill

31

Columbia

50

Franklin

Co
Gr

65

Natchez Trace Parkway

20

Summertown

Ethridge

64

Culleoka

373

64

Lawrenceburg

Pulaski

Adamsville   Crum

22

Shiloh

142

Savannah

128

Pickwick Dam

57

Counce

West Day Trip 2

ALABAMA

open to the public. (She is also there for autographs on scheduled dates.) Open daily April through October, and from the middle of November to the first part of January; closed Thanksgiving, Christmas Eve, Christmas Day, and New Year's Day. No charge to enter the ranch; fee for tours, camping, and other activities. (931) 296-7700; www.lorettalynn.com.

NATCHEZ TRACE STATE PARK

Get back on I-40 west, crossing the Tennessee River, to get to Wildersville and Natchez Trace State Forest, which covers 48,000 acres, and Natchez Trace State Park. Named for the well-known Natchez Trace—the Nashville to Natchez, Mississippi, trail of the eighteenth and nineteenth centuries (see SOUTHWEST, DAY TRIP 1)—the park once contained some of the most heavily abused and eroded land in Tennessee. In the 1930s, the U.S. Department of Agriculture acquired the acreage and set up a "Land-Use-Area" project that showed how damaged wasteland could be made productive again.

Today, the park has beautiful woodlands to explore in addition to four lakes with fishing and boating, a swimming beach, cabins, playgrounds, picnic areas, hiking trails, off-road vehicle trails, firing and archery ranges, and four campgrounds with 210 sites. The Red Leaves Overnight Trail allows those who are interested to hike into camp, but a backcountry permit must be obtained before starting out. And the park is one of only two sites in the state with a wrangler camp, which means you can bring your horse along with your tent. The park rents quarter horses for guided trail rides.

Natchez Trace recently underwent a massive $10 million renovation that added new cabins and upgraded those that were already there. A new campground, wrangler camp, and equestrian center (opened in 2004) were built, and more rooms and meeting space were added to Pin Oak Lodge, which was also renovated (see "Where to Stay") along with the group lodge.

The world's third-largest pecan tree is located here, and photos of the tree's growth are on display in the park visitor center. There is a park store and service station on the grounds. Open year-round. There is no entrance fee, but there is a charge for camping and cabins. For additional information, write to Natchez Trace Information Center, Wildersville, TN 38388; call (800) 250–8616 or (901) 968–3742; or visit www.state.tn.us/environment/parks/parks/NatchezTrace.

WHERE TO STAY

Pin Oak Lodge. Natchez Trace State Park, Wildersville. The attractive lodge sits on Pin Oak Lake and offers forty-seven rooms, a large restaurant, a recreation room, a playground, tennis courts, and a swimming pool. Reservations recommended. Open March through November. $$. (901) 968–8176 or (800) 250–8616.

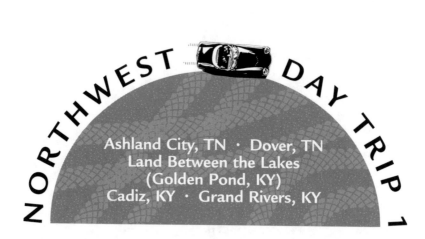

ASHLAND CITY

Located on the Cumberland River, Ashland City is best reached by taking TN-12 (also called Ashland City Highway) north for approximately 20 miles. Nashvillians know it as a place to get tasty fried catfish, and a number of restaurants there specialize in these popular critters. The Cumberland River and nearby Cheatham Lake attract fishermen for the crappie, largemouth bass, sauger, rockfish, and catfish found in the waters, and Cheatham Wildlife Management Area, a hunter's haven during certain months, is perfect for bird-watching and observing other wild animals. The Cumberland River Bicentennial Trail has turned a railroad bed into a 3.7-mile trail that winds north along the Cumberland River and can be used for walking, jogging, bicycling, riding horses, and nature watching. Call (615) 792-4211 for more information, or visit www.cheatham chamber.org/trail.

WHERE TO EAT

Bill's Catfish. 1205 Hydes Ferry Pike (just off TN-12). Bill's has been a mainstay in Ashland City for more than twenty-five years and was resurrected several years back after a fire gutted the place. If you like fried catfish, this place does it right, with accompaniments such as white beans, hush puppies, and tasty slaw. Other menu items include pit barbecue, fried chicken, oysters, shrimp, steak, country ham, burgers, and a few grilled items. Plate lunches are served for the noontime meal, with

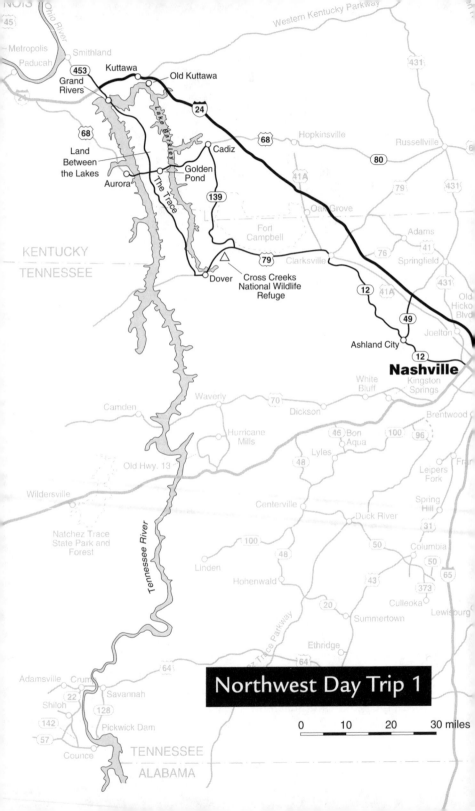

Northwest Day Trip 1

0   10   20   30 miles

a choice of meat and three vegetables as well as a lunch buffet. A banquet room is available. Open for lunch and dinner Tuesday through Sunday. $-$$. (615) 792-9193.

Dozier's. 1190 Dozier Boat Dock Road (off TN-49 west). Probably the city's oldest catfish restaurant, Dozier's is situated at the mouth of the Harpeth River. The setting is quiet, and there's a picnic table if you want to enjoy the surroundings. Catfish, with the requisite hush puppies and slaw, is what the restaurant is known for, but diners also can order fried oysters, chicken, and hamburger steaks. Open daily for dinner; lunch on Saturday and Sunday. $$; credit cards not accepted. (615) 792-9175.

Riverview Restaurant and Marina. 110 Old River Road. While enjoying a view of the Cumberland River, diners here can munch on catfish, shrimp, and even crab legs. The eatery serves a luncheon buffet with traditional country cooking and also opens its doors for the morning crowd. Open for all three meals Tuesday through Sunday. $-$$. (615) 792-7358.

DOVER

Continue on TN-12 until you reach Clarksville. Follow US-79 west to Dover. The small town is at the southern entrance to the Tennessee Valley Authority's Land Between the Lakes.

WHERE TO GO

Cross Creeks National Wildlife Refuge. TN-49 south. This national wildlife refuge stretches 12 miles on either side of the Cumberland River between Dover and Cumberland City. Its 8,862 acres of marsh, farmland, and hardwood forests are managed to provide feeding and resting habitat for migrating waterfowl. In the winter thousands of ducks and geese glide on the water, and a number of bald eagles nest there. There is seasonal fishing, hunting, and wildlife observation. At the visitor center, nature lovers will find exhibits, audiovisual presentations, and an observation window. Open mid-March through October; call for hours. Free. (931) 232-7477; www.crosscreeks.fws.gov.

Fort Donelson National Battlefield. US-79 west. When Fort Donelson was captured in 1862, this was the North's first major victory of the Civil War. It was after this winter battle that the South was forced to give up Southern Kentucky and much of Middle and West Tennessee, opening the way for the Union forces. Sites at the park include the Confederate Monument, river batteries, the Dover Hotel (one of the four buildings that survived the Battle of Dover and the only existing original structure in which a major surrender took place), Fort Donelson, and the National Cemetery, which holds more than 600 Civil War–era graves. The sites can be seen by taking the 6-mile self-guided auto tour. The visitor center presents an audiovisual program and contains exhibits pertaining to the battle. Open daily year-round except Christmas. The Dover Hotel is only open during the summer months. Free. (931) 232-5706; www.nps.gov/fodo.

WHERE TO STAY AND EAT

Riverfront Plantation Inn. 190 Crow Lane. This twenty-acre waterfront estate—a restored Civil War–era home—is adjacent to Fort Donelson, with a view of the Cumberland River. Five guest rooms, all with private baths, have fireplaces and screened-in porches. In-room coffee is available. Travelers can enjoy a gourmet plantation-style breakfast or a country-style spread. Breakfast, brunch, lunch, and evening meals are offered with advance reservations to inn guests and others ($$-$$$). Riverfront Plantation also pampers lodgers with turn-down service, complete with chocolates, by request. $$-$$$. (931) 232-9492; www.riverfrontplantation.com.

LAND BETWEEN THE LAKES

Take US-79 west from Dover until you reach The Trace. This is the 40-mile-long artery through the finger of land between Kentucky Lake and Lake Barkley. Access to camping areas, boat docks, picnic facilities, visitor centers, and other sites in the recreation area is available off The Trace.

WHERE TO GO

Land Between the Lakes. This area is managed by the Tennessee Valley Authority and is a wooded peninsula bordered on three sides by water (with more than 300 miles of undeveloped shoreline). This national recreation and environmental education area harbors a rich variety of animal life, including fish, buffalo, whitetail deer, owls, wild turkeys, beaver, eagles, and bobcats. It is a popular spot for backpacking, hiking, bicycling, hunting, and camping, with several hundred campsites for both tents and RVs, and one even geared for those on horseback. Organized education and recreation groups can use the group camps, which have dormitory-style housing, cafeterias, and other amenities, and there are also large campsites for groups that can be reserved.

The best place to start your visit to Land Between the Lakes (LBL) is the Golden Pond Visitor Center. Here you can get an overview of the recreational opportunities in the 170,000-acre expanse, browse the gift shop with regional crafts, and see the planetarium. Be sure to pick up a calendar of events with a schedule of the daily activities, which range from a wetlands walk to feeding time with the eagles to a butter-making demonstration. Stargazing, canoe trips, ice-cream making, and even a national butterfly counting weekend are some of the other interesting programs at Land Between the Lakes. Many of the animal programs are staged at the Nature Station, where another gift shop is located. The Nature Station, a fun place for kids to experience wildlife up close, is open March through November; special winter trips are scheduled to see migratory waterfowl and eagles.

The Homeplace—1850 is a living history farm, reconstructed to portray the way life was for the people who settled the land between the Tennessee and Cumberland Rivers during the first half of the nineteenth century. Historic interpreters tend to daily chores in a setting of sixteen original log structures, and special events are staged here in June and September (see "Festivals and Celebrations"). The Homeplace is open March through November and requires an admission fee. There is a gift shop here as well.

Visitors can also view a 750-acre native prairie habitat at the Elk and Bison Prairie. Bison, elk, and other wildlife can be seen from the comfort of your car if you take the 3½-mile auto tour that allows safe

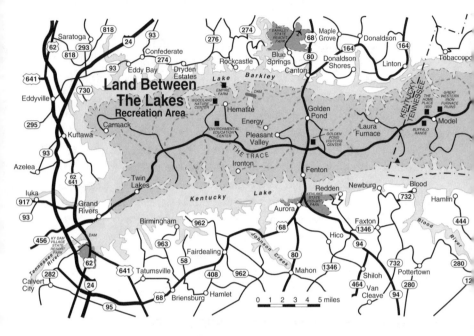

access to these animals. Guided van trips are also available through the Nature Station. Open year-round. Fee.

LBL rents bicycles, mountain bikes, canoes, and paddleboats to visitors, too. For more information, contact Tennessee Valley Authority, Land Between the Lakes, 100 Van Morgan Drive, Golden Pond, KY 42211, or call (800) LBL–7077 or (270) 924–2000. You can also take a virtual tour of LBL at www.lbl.org.

WHERE TO EAT

Brass Lantern. 16593 US–68/KY–80 (just 5 miles west of The Trace), Aurora. If hunger pangs strike anytime after 5:00 P.M., you should make a point to visit this cozy eatery, which has been open since 1972. Five dining areas combine rough cedar walls, brick floors, and strings of white lights to give Brass Lantern its pleasant ambience. Add to that delicious charbroiled steaks, pork chops, lobster tail, and daily specials, and it's easy to see why this restaurant is so popular. The entire place is one big gift shop, too, with unique

silver jewelry, handbags, belts, collectibles, and pottery. Open most evenings from March through December. Reservations suggested. $$-$$$. (800) 474-2770 or (270) 474-2773; www.brasslanternrestaurant.com.

CADIZ

To reach Cadiz, travel east on US-68/KY-80. This small town is the eastern access to Land Between the Lakes, and there are several privately owned marinas and resorts in the area. Cadiz has some wonderful Victorian homes on Main Street as well as several antiques malls downtown. The Trigg County Ham Festival is a popular celebration each October that honors the award-winning Broadbent ham (see "Festivals and Celebrations").

WHERE TO GO

Cadiz–Trigg County Tourist Commission. 22 Main Street. The welcome center, housed in an 1867 log cabin, can provide you with information about the area. Open Monday through Friday. (270) 522-3892. Another welcome center, which is open Monday through Saturday, is located on US-68/KY-80 (exit 65 off I-24); www.go cadiz.com.

WHERE TO STAY AND EAT

Lake Barkley State Resort. The resort is 29 miles west of Hopkinsville, Kentucky (off KY-1489). Take US-68 west to KY-1489. This is the only three-star-rated resort in Kentucky. Situated on the shores of Lake Barkley, the 3,600-acre park offers camping, boating, fishing, golf, swimming, tennis, a trap range, hiking trails, playgrounds, picnic facilities, a game room, a fitness center, cottages, a convention center, and a popular open-beamed lodge that is worth a stop even if you're not spending the night. The beautiful building is constructed of western cedar, Douglas fir, and nearly four acres of glass and was renovated in 1998. Most of the 120 rooms and four suites offer a lake view, and the dining room overlooks the swimming pool and the lake. The gift shop carries a good selection of Kentucky crafts.

A hearty buffet is usually offered for each meal, or diners can order off the varied menu. Traditional breakfast items are available in the morning, and the lunch and dinner menus include salads, sandwiches, and entrees such as steak and shrimp. Open daily. $-$$.

The Little River Lodge provides ten rooms and one suite and can be rented as a whole unit. The park hosts special events throughout the year, such as the Eagles Weekend in February and a 5K Run in October. $-$$$. (800) 325-1708 or (270) 924-1131; www.state.ky.us /agencies/parks/lakebark.htm.

GRAND RIVERS

From Cadiz, you can either backtrack to The Trace to reach Grand Rivers or head up on I-24 west and get off at exit 31. Take KY-453 south for about 4 miles to get to town. Grand Rivers is at the north end of the Land Between the Lakes area and is close to Barkley Dam and other private and state resort parks. There are a few antiques stores in Grand Rivers, many operating seasonally.

WHERE TO EAT

Mr. Bill's, Patti's Restaurant, and Miss Patti's Iron Kettle. 1793 J. H. O'Bryan Avenue. One of Western Kentucky's best-known eateries, this restaurant also has been written up in *Bon Appétit*, *The Milwaukee Sentinel*, and the *Tucson Citizen*. The restaurant combines two previously separate establishments, Mr. Bill's and Patti's. Patti's is famous for 2-inch-thick charbroiled pork chops, "sky-high" meringue pies, and flowerpot bread with whipped strawberry butter, but you might also want to try one of the sandwiches, steaks, or specially seasoned burgers. Patti's Sawdust Pie—with coconut, pecans, graham cracker crumbs, bananas, and whipped cream—is one of the dining spot's most popular desserts. The Iron Kettle opened in 1998 and is best known for its Sunday brunch, with Belgian waffles and made-to-order omelets. Five gift shops also operate on the property in old log cabins full of trinkets and country crafts, and you can play eighteen-hole miniature golf. The restaurant offers VIP service from the local airport and any of the nearby marinas and hotels. Open daily for lunch and dinner except for four days at Christmas. Reservations suggested. $-$$. (270) 362-8844, (270) 362-0409, or (888) 736-2515; www.pattis-settlement.com.

WHERE TO STAY

The Davis House Bed and Breakfast. 528 Willow Way (off US-62, about 12 miles from Grand Rivers), Kuttawa. This pleasant home is more than one hundred years old and located on Lake Barkley in the town of Kuttawa, an Indian word meaning "beautiful." Hardwood floors, original fireplaces, and antique furnishings add to the charm. Guests will find five guest rooms with shared baths and a full country-style breakfast. Rental boats and boat docking facilities are also available. $$; credit cards not accepted. (270) 388-4468; www.thedavishouse.com.

Silver Cliff Inn Bed and Breakfast. 1980 Lake Barkley Drive, Old Kuttawa. Nine miles from Grand Rivers sits a large Victorian mansion built near Lake Barkley in 1874. Now an inn, it has six guest rooms furnished with antiques and private baths. You can relax downstairs on the front porch or upstairs on the wraparound deck while you admire the surrounding gardens. Silver Cliff is across the street from the Old Kuttawa Beach and Park. A full country-gourmet breakfast is offered. The inn is available for meetings, receptions, and catered brunches or lunches. You can also rent the whole house (two-night minimum) and "be your own host" for family reunions. $$; credit cards not accepted. (270) 388-5858; www.kentuckylake.com/silvercliff.

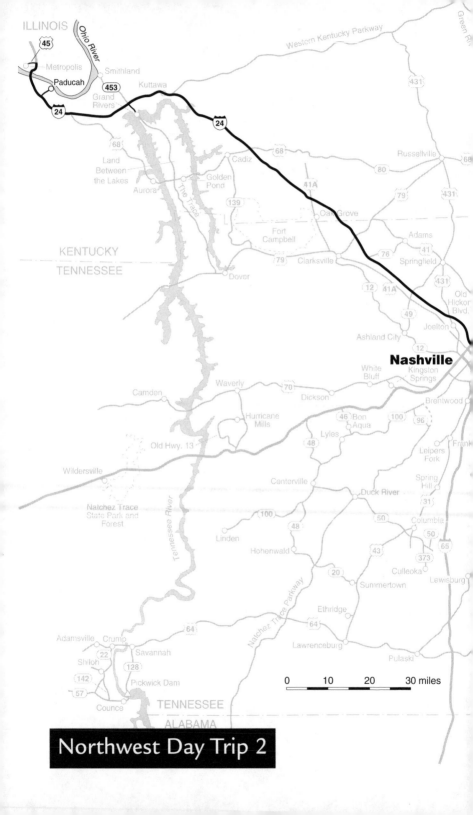

Northwest Day Trip 2

PADUCAH

The most direct route to Paducah is to take I-24 west. The city, which sits on the Ohio River, is about 140 miles from Nashville. If you're heading there from Grand Rivers, Kentucky (see NORTH-WEST, DAY TRIP 1), take KY-453 north to I-24.

History tells us that in 1827 General William Clark bought some 37,000 acres of Western Kentucky land for $5.00. The area included a town called Pekin, and Clark renamed it Paducah. There's some wonderful architecture in the city's older structures. A downtown walking tour includes the magnificent Irvin Cobb building and the Old National Bank Building. Pick up a brochure from the tourist commission to guide you. For a glimpse of the river, drive or walk behind the seawall downtown, sit on one of the benches, and watch the barges go by. You can see Paducah's history come alive in the flood-wall murals by artist Robert Dafford.

This Ohio River town packs the people in each spring with the annual Dogwood Festival, which showcases the thousands of blooming dogwoods in Paducah (see "Festivals and Celebrations," under April). The American Quilter's Society National Quilt Show is held in conjunction with the Dogwood Festival.

WHERE TO GO

Paducah–McCracken County Convention and Visitors Bureau. 128 Broadway. The Visitors Bureau is conveniently located downtown and is open Monday through Friday. (800) PADUCAH or (270) 443–8783; www.paducah-tourism.org.

Bob Noble Park. 2915 Park Avenue. The main reason for stopping at this 135-acre park is to see the massive carved Indian *Wacinton,* created by sculptor Peter Toth. The wooden figure honors the Chickasaw Indians, who lived and hunted in the area. Kentucky is the forty-sixth state to have an Indian monument by the artist. There are concerts in the park on Friday evening during the summer. Open year-round. Free. (270) 444–8533.

Harrah's Bluegrass Downs. 150 Downs Drive. Kentucky being horse country, it's not unusual to find horse racing in Paducah. Harrah's Bluegrass Downs is the site for harness racing from September through most of October (but call for a schedule). An enclosed clubhouse and lounge with simulcast betting on races at other Kentucky Thoroughbred tracks are open year-round. You can also stop by most mornings to see the horses work out on the track. Fee. (270) 444–7117.

The Market House. 200 Broadway. Built in 1905, the present Market House has been restored as a center for the arts. Three orga-

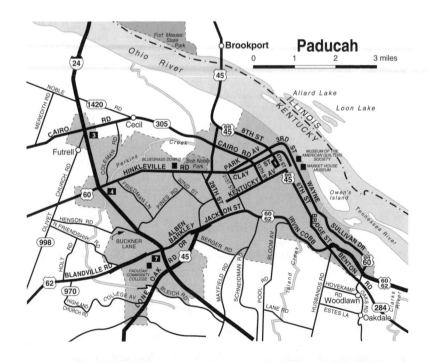

nizations now make their home here, including the Yeiser Art Center, William Clark Market House Museum, and Market House Theatre.

Yeiser Art Center contains a permanent collection of nineteenth- and twentieth-century artwork and also rotates exhibitions by regional, national, and international artists. Lectures, workshops, classes, and other activities are offered during the year. Open Tuesday through Saturday. Fee. (270) 442-2453.

William Clark Market House Museum gives visitors a glimpse into Paducah's past, with exhibits on native sons Alben W. Barkley and author-humorist Irvin S. Cobb. The first motorized fire truck is on display here, as is the complete interior of the circa 1870 List Drug Store, which was moved piece by piece into the museum. Other things to see include antique furniture, glassware, clothing, quilts, tools, and Indian artifacts. Open Tuesday through Saturday, March through December; closed during January and February. Closed on major holidays. Fee. (270) 443-7759.

Market House Theatre is a leading community theater in Kentucky. The company produces six shows a year, ranging from classics to Broadway plays to original works. Market House Theatre also does vaudeville, children's productions, and dinner theater. The public is invited to tour the facility Tuesday through Friday. Free. (270) 444-6828; www.mhtplay.com.

Museum of the American Quilter's Society. 215 Jefferson Street. The quilts displayed here range from an antique Amish covering to a contemporary piece that looks more like a painting. Three galleries in this 30,000-square-foot museum display both a permanent collection (with more than 200 quilts) and traveling exhibits that feature the work of quilters from all over the country. Quilters and those interested in the art will love the extensive selection of books on the subject. Throughout the year, there are guest quilt makers, workshops, and seminars. The society sponsors a National Quilt Show each year at the Julian Carroll Convention Center. Open year-round Monday through Saturday; Sunday afternoon from April through October. Fee. (270) 442-8856; www.quiltmuseum.org.

Paducah Wall to Wall: Portraits of Our Past. These murals are located at the foot of Broadway downtown, on the flood wall by the Ohio River. For a visual tour of Paducah's past, don't miss this series of colorful 15-foot-tall murals by Louisiana artist Robert Dafford, that showcases the city's history in twenty-eight different painted sections. Don't miss the annual Festival of Murals (see "Festivals and Celebrations," under June). Open daily. Free.

River Heritage Museum. 117 South Water Street. Located in a historic building downtown, this museum features exhibits that tell the story of the region around the Ohio, Tennessee, Cumberland, and Mississippi Rivers. The museum also incorporates the Maiden Alley Cinema, which shows newly released art films and independent films on the weekends, and the Founders Room, which features period furniture and objects from the mid-nineteenth century. Open daily. Fee. (270) 575-9958; www.riverheritagemuseum.org.

Whitehaven. 1845 Lone Oak Road. This 1860s mansion now serves as a state tourist welcome center, where visitors can obtain information about this part of Kentucky. Memorabilia of former vice president Alben W. Barkley are on view in second-floor displays. Tours are offered daily; call ahead for hours. Free. (270) 554-2077.

WHERE TO EAT

C.C. Cohen. 103 Market House Square. This eatery, situated in the historic Cohen building, delivers seafood, prime rib, steaks, salads, and gourmet burgers in the heart of downtown Paducah. Open for lunch and dinner Monday through Saturday. $$. (270) 442-6391.

Cynthia's Ristorante. 127 Market House Square. Cynthia's features Northern Italian food, with entrees such as homemade pasta, veal chops, seafood, quail, lamb, and a grilled mozzarella salad. The menu changes weekly, so you'll find something new all the time. The strawberry crepes are one of the popular gourmet desserts. Open Tuesday through Saturday for dinner. $$-$$$. (270) 443-3319; www.cynthiasristorante.com.

The Holman House Cafeteria. 3333 Irvin Cobb Drive. This restaurant serves a buffet-style meal with Southern specialties as well as a variety of sandwiches. The "mile-high" meringue pies made in-house are worth a stop if you just want something sweet. Open for lunch and dinner Monday through Saturday. $$. (270) 442-9784.

Jeremiah's Froghead Brewery. 225 Broadway. Jeremiah's is the home of the twenty-ounce steak, which will more than satisfy any meat lover. The restaurant, which is located in two historic bank buildings, also serves frogs legs and has an extensive list of appetizers. The microbrewery churns out handcrafted beers and ales to drink with your dinner. Open Monday through Saturday for dinner. $$-$$$. (270) 443-3991.

Kountry Kastle Barbecue. 3415 Clarks River Road. Barbecued pork, beef, mutton, ribs, and chicken can be found at this barbecue joint, which has been operating since 1939. Order a slab of ribs, half a chicken, pork by the pound, or a mutton sandwich if you have a hankering for some 'cue. $-$$. (270) 443-9978.

Max's Brick Oven Café. 112 Market House Square. You'll find everything from pizzas to lamb, sandwiches to seafood to pasta at this spot. Open for dinner only Monday through Saturday, reservations suggested. $$. (270) 575-3473.

Tribeca Mexican Cuisine. 127 Market House Square. Serving authentic Mexican food, Tribeca is open for lunch and dinner Tuesday through Saturday. $$. (270) 444-3960.

The Whaler's Catch Restaurant and Oyster Bar. 123 North Second Street. Raw oysters and fresh seafood reel diners into the Whaler's Catch. Cajun-style entrees and boiled shrimp have become popular choices here. A seafood market operates next door if you want to take some for the road. Open for lunch and dinner Monday through Saturday. $$. (270) 444-7701.

WHERE TO STAY

Fisher Mansion Bed and Breakfast. 901 Jefferson Street. Located in the historic Lower Town District, this Queen Anne–style mansion offers four guest rooms with private baths. A full Southern breakfast is served in the dining room or outdoors in the courtyard in good weather. This B&B offers elopement weekend specials. $$-$$$. (270) 443-0716; www.paducah-lodging.com.

Fox Briar Farm Inn. 515 Schmidt Road. This inn, which is situated on a hundred-acre wooded site overlooking a scenic lake, offers nine guest rooms with private baths. There's also a huge covered porch to enjoy as well as a full gourmet breakfast in the morning. No smoking, pets, children, or alcohol. $$-$$$. (270) 554-1774 or (888) FOXBRIAR.

J.R.'s Executive Inn Riverfront. 1 Executive Boulevard. This is Paducah's largest hotel, situated on the banks of the Ohio River. There are more than 400 guest rooms, including 35 riverfront suites. The Julian Carroll Convention Center is at one end of the inn, and on weekends the hotel's Showroom Lounge features big-name entertainers including Tanya Tucker, Billy Dean, and Ray Stevens. An Olympic-size indoor pool, a game room, two full-service restaurants, two lounges, and the Galleria shopping area round out the Executive Inn's amenities. Ask about the Riverboat Package, which includes tickets for Harrah's Riverboat Casino in Metropolis, Illinois. $$. (800) 866–3636 or (270) 443–8000; www.jrsexecutiveinn.com.

Paducah Harbor Plaza Bed and Breakfast. 201 Broadway. Part of this five-story building a block from the Ohio River is a bed-and-breakfast, with four guest rooms, some with private baths and one with a fireplace, located on the second floor. Handmade quilts and antiques accent the 10-foot ceilings, tongue-and-groove painted floors, and transoms in the rooms, providing cozy surroundings for a stay in Paducah. A continental breakfast with added items such as sausage balls and quiche is served. A kitchen is also available for guests. $$. (800) 719–7799 or (270) 442–2698; www.phplaza.com.

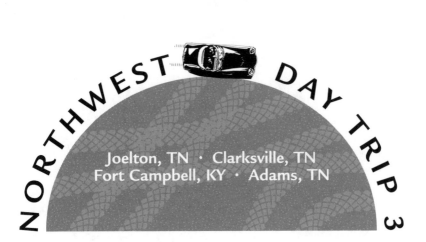

It's a pleasant drive to this part of the state on US–41A. You can also zip up there on I–24 west. If you take the interstate, you might want to go to Adams first, see Clarksville and Fort Campbell, and then head back to Nashville on US–41A.

JOELTON

The town of Joelton, located northwest of downtown Nashville, is considered a suburb of Music City, with many residents opting for the benefits of small-town living while being close enough to the perks of the larger metropolis. The superb dining at Shadowbrook is the real draw.

WHERE TO EAT

Shadowbrook. 5397 Rawlings Road. Private dining by appointment has never been finer than at Shadowbrook. You can easily forget you are in the hills of Tennessee when you drive up to this attractive Tudor mansion, which sits on Lake Marrowbone. The house has been in the Rawlings family since it was erected in 1929, inspired by the years the late A. L. Rawlings spent at the University of Edinburgh in Scotland. The structure is built of native stone and massive hand-hewn virgin timbers. Visitors who dine here relax in an elegant dining room, appointed with china, crystal, and flowers and surrounded by family heirlooms. Shadowbrook serves a selection of

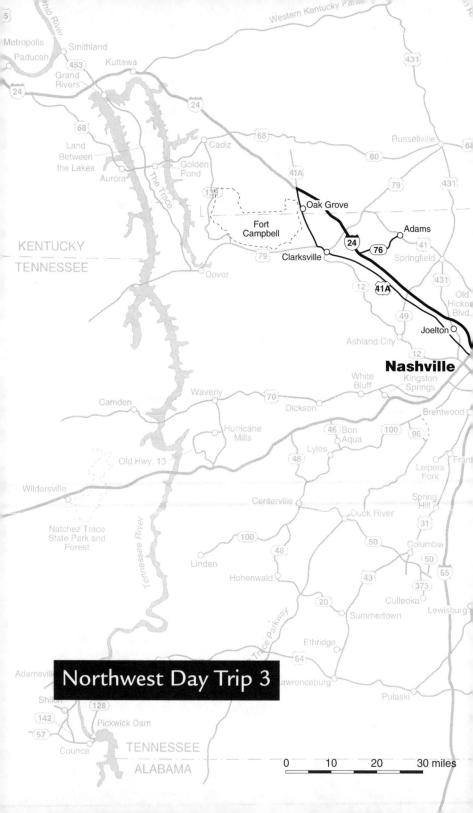

Northwest Day Trip 3

courses, depending on what you choose in advance. The beef tenderloin Southern Elegance Dinner is a popular choice, complete with delicious accompaniments. Owner Clara Davenport always has one of her special homemade desserts to complete the generous meal, and husband Nelson is more than happy to show off their extensive Eskimo art collection. Shadowbrook is a popular spot for meetings, receptions, and parties, and reservations must be made well in advance. Open by appointment. $$$; cash only. (615) 876-0700.

CLARKSVILLE

Continue west on US-41A to Clarksville. The city, founded in 1784, is Tennessee's fifth largest municipality, supporting a population of some 210,000 residents. Farming plays a large role here, with tobacco serving as a major source of income for the area. Both the Cumberland and Red Rivers run through Clarksville, which is why it is sometimes referred to as "Queen City of the Cumberland." The newly constructed RiverWalk snakes around the Cumberland River, providing a pleasant place for a stroll. Austin Peay State University is located here, and its Center for Creative Arts schedules a variety of concerts, dance and theatrical performances, art exhibitions, and musical productions throughout the year.

Clarksville is rich in historic architecture, and visitors can take either a 14-mile driving tour of the area or a 2-mile walking tour of downtown. Downtown Clarksville was hit hard by the January 1999 tornado. Although some of the historic buildings have been restored, others had to be demolished. (Pick up a brochure at the Clarksville–Montgomery County Tourist Information Center.) The Old-Time Fiddlers' Championship takes place here each March (see "Festivals and Celebrations").

WHERE TO GO

Clarksville–Montgomery County Tourist Information Center. 180 Holiday Road (off I-24 at exit 4). You can find numerous brochures here on things to do in the area. Open daily. (931) 553-8467.

Beachaven Vineyards and Winery. 1100 Dunlop Lane (off I-24 at exit 4). Judge William O. Beach opened the doors to his winery in 1987 after spending twenty-five years as an amateur wine maker. Visitors can tour the two acres of grapes and see the wine-making process firsthand. Free samples of Beachaven's award-winning spirits are available in the Tudor-style building, along with gifts and wine accessories. From May to October, the winery stages free evening concerts on the grounds and sells bottles of iced wines for picnickers. Open daily. Free. (931) 645-8867; www.beachavenwinery.com.

Customs House Museum and Cultural Center. 200 South Second Street. This local museum is a good place to start a visit to Clarksville. The building itself—erected in 1898 as a post office—is fabulous, with its Italianate ornamentation, slate roof, copper eagles, and Romanesque arches. Inside, travelers will find various historical and local history exhibits. A three-story addition increased gallery space and includes an auditorium, classrooms, a collections laboratory, offices, and a museum store. Traveling art and science exhibitions also are scheduled throughout the year. Open daily except Monday. Fee. (931) 648-5780; www.customshousemuseum.org.

Dunbar Cave State Natural Area. 401 Dunbar Cave Road (4 miles off US-41A). This 8-mile cave, inhabited by prehistoric Indians some 10,000 years ago, is part of the 110-acre natural area. At the turn of the century, the cave was a mineral springs resort where wealthy people came to bathe in the healing waters. Later, in the 1930s, big band concerts were held at the mouth of the cavern. And when Grand Ole Opry star Roy Acuff owned it from the 1940s to the 1960s, the cave was the site of country music shows. A sixty-minute guided tour takes visitors about a half mile into the cavern. There are also foot trails, fishing, and year-round educational programs. An old bathhouse now serves as a visitor center and museum. Call ahead for a schedule of cave tours (reservations and flashlights—nominal fee required). Free. (931) 648-5526; www.state.tn.us/environment/parks/parks/DunbarCave.

Queen of Clarksville. McGregor Park on Riverside Drive. Board the *Queen of Clarksville* paddle-wheel boat for a sightseeing tour down the Cumberland River. The ninety-minute cruise enlightens passengers with sights and historical information along the way. Dinner and dance cruises are offered on the 150-passenger boat, plus the paddle wheeler also travels to Dover in the late summer. Open April through October. Fee. (931) 647-5500.

The Roxy Regional Theatre. 100 Franklin Street. A major renovation of this two-level 168-seat facility took place in 1995, adding a theatrical venue to downtown Clarksville. The regional theater presents premieres, new versions of classics, musicals, and other performances on weekends. Fee. (931) 645-7699; www.roxyregionaltheatre.org.

WHERE TO EAT

Hachland Hall. 1601 Madison Street. Hungry guests will find a variety of delicious meals available at Hachland Hall, ranging from Southern fried chicken to Moroccan leg of lamb. For more than forty years, owner and chef Phila Hach has been catering to people from around the world at her historic house and inn located in the heart of Clarksville (see "Where to Stay"). The lovely restaurant can serve up to 350 in the grand ballroom, and other dining areas overlook a bird sanctuary and wildflower gardens. Reservations required. Open for breakfast, lunch, and dinner. $$-$$$. (931) 647-4084.

Red's Bakery and Delicatessen. 101 Riverside Drive. A hearty breakfast can be had here anytime, but it's also a good place to order a deli sandwich on homemade bread. This unassuming restaurant also prepares barbecue chicken, hot roast beef and vegetables, and other plate lunches. It's hard to pass on "Red's Famous Potato," a twice-baked spud topped with melted American cheese, or the assorted cakes, pies, and other pastries, all made in-house. Open for all three meals, Monday through Saturday. $; credit cards not accepted. (931) 647-5646.

Charlie's Steak House. US–41A, Oak Grove, KY. This old-time restaurant has been drawing diners since 1952. Charlie's is a meat-eater's place, known for its delicious steaks. Customers will also find burgers, seafood, hefty baked potatoes, and salads. Open Monday through Saturday for dinner. $-$$; credit cards are not accepted, but personal checks are. (270) 439-4592.

WHERE TO STAY

Hachland Hall. 1601 Madison Street. Lodging facilities here range from three log cottages built in the late 1700s to six antiques-filled rooms in the main inn. One of the cabins is called the "Honeymoon Cottage," complete with love poems and other romantic memorabilia. Rooms in the inn are furnished with four-poster beds and handmade quilts. Hachland Hall serves a full, plantation-style breakfast in the morning, but the meal is not included in the lodging price. $$. (931) 647–4084.

FORT CAMPBELL

US-41A takes you on up to Fort Campbell, which is home to a 100,000-acre military reservation straddling both Tennessee and Kentucky. The well-known Army base is the home of the 101st Airborne Division–Air Assault—the one generally called up first to head overseas during a major crisis.

WHERE TO GO

Don F. Pratt Memorial Museum. Twenty-sixth Street and Tennessee Avenue, Building 5702. Exhibits in this museum, which opened in 1956, depict the history of the 101st Airborne "Screaming Eagles" from World War II to the present. Displays include a restored WWII cargo glider, items belonging to Adolph Hitler and other Nazi officials, two seventeenth-century bronze eagles, captured enemy weapons and equipment, and other military items. Ambitious plans are in the works to move and expand the museum, including adding an IMAX theater. An opening date is scheduled for 2007. Open daily except Christmas and New Year's Day. There is also a gift shop. Guests must register their vehicles at the visitor center, Gate 4, off US-41A. Free. (270) 798–4986; www.campbell.army.mil/pratt/index.html.

ADAMS

Take TN-76 east or exit 11 off I-24 to reach this small bewitching town. Adams is synonymous with the Bell Witch, the legendary sorceress who tormented the Bell family for years. The story may be the most documented account of the supernatural in this country, with many books written about the hauntings. During July folks gather in Adams for the old-time threshing show, to see displays of wheat-threshing equipment and various demonstrations and events. There's also the Bell Witch Bluegrass Festival in August (see "Festivals and Celebrations").

WHERE TO GO

Adams Jamboree. US-41. The old Bell schoolhouse is the place to hear country music in these parts. Entertainment ranges from youngsters taking the stage with their guitars to more seasoned musicians. Every Saturday night. Fee. (615) 696-2593.

Bell Witch Cave. 129 Eden Road. The cave where the infamous witch hung out is now privately owned, but daily guided tours are offered May through October and for larger groups by appointment. Fee. (615) 696-3055.

Port Royal State Park. 3300 Old Clarksville Highway (off TN-76, 8 miles from Adams). During the 1800s, Port Royal was a thriving town on the Red River and a place where steamboats and flatboats carrying farm items and produce would depart for destinations farther north. The town faded with the advent of train travel, and now a thirty-acre state park remains. A covered bridge built in 1955, which served as the area's centerpiece, was damaged in a flood in 1998, leaving half of the bridge in place. Picnic facilities, nature trails, and river access for canoeists and fishermen are also available. And a small museum covers the history of the Port Royal area. Open daily. Free. (931) 358-9696; www.state.tn.us/ environment/parks/parks/PortRoyal.

Regional
Information

Day Trip 1
Goodlettsville Chamber of Commerce
100 South Main Street
Goodlettsville, TN 37072
(615) 859-7979
www.goodlettsvillechamber.com

Logan County Chamber of Commerce
116 South Main Street
Russellville, KY 42276
(270) 726-2206
www.loganchamber.com

Bowling Green Area Convention
and Visitors Bureau
352 Three Springs Road
Bowling Green, KY 42104
(800) 326-7465 or (270) 782-0800
www.bg.ky.net/tourism

Day Trip 2
Cave City Tourist Convention Center
502 Mammoth Cave Street
Cave City, KY 42127
(800) 346-8908 or (270) 773-3131
www.cavecity.com

Day Trip 3
LaRue County Chamber of Commerce
58 Lincoln Square
Hodgenville, KY 42748
(270) 358-3411
www.laruecountychamber.org

Bardstown-Nelson County Tourist Commission
107 East Stephen Foster Avenue
Bardstown, KY 40004
(800) 638-4877 or (502) 348-4877
www.visitbardstown.com/tourism

NORTHEAST

Day Trip 1
Gaylord Opryland Resort and Convention Center
2808 Opryland Drive
Nashville, TN 37214
(615) 889-6611
www.gaylordhotels.com/gaylordopryland

Day Trip 2
Hendersonville Area Chamber of Commerce
101 Wessington Place
Hendersonville, TN 37075
(615) 824-2818
www.hendersonvillechamber.com

Gallatin Chamber of Commerce
118 West Main Street
Gallatin, TN 37066
(615) 452-4000
www.gallatintn.org

Sumner County Tourism
118 West Main Street
Gallatin, TN 37066
(615) 230–8474
www.sumnercountytourism.com

Day Trip 3
City Hall of Red Boiling Springs
166 Dale Street
Red Boiling Springs, TN 37150
(615) 699–2011
www.redboilingspringstn.com

Day Trip 4
Jamestown–Fentress County Chamber of Commerce
Courthouse Square
Jamestown, TN 38556
(800) 327–3945 or (931) 879–9948
www.jamestowntn.org

Historic Rugby, Inc.
P.O. Box 8
Rugby, TN 37733
(423) 628–2441
www.historicrugby.org

EAST

Day Trip 1
The Hermitage
4580 Rachel's Lane
Hermitage, TN 37076
(615) 889–2941
www.thehermitage.com

Day Trip 2
Lebanon–Wilson County Chamber of Commerce
149 Public Square
Lebanon, TN 37087
(615) 444-5503
www.wilsoncounty.com/lebanonchamber

Watertown Business Association
116 Depot Street
Watertown, TN 37184
(615) 237-0270

Smithville–DeKalb County Chamber of Commerce
210 East Public Square
Smithville, TN 37166
(615) 597-4163
www.smithvilletn.com and www.dekalbtn.com

Day Trip 3
Cookeville–Putnam County Chamber of Commerce
One Town Center, 1 West First Street
Cookeville, TN 38501
(800) 264-5541 or (931) 526-2211
www.cookevillechamber.com

Greater Cumberland County Chamber of Commerce
34 South Main Street
Crossville, TN 38555
(931) 484-8444
www.crossville-chamber.com

SOUTHEAST

Day Trip 1
Rutherford County Chamber of Commerce
501 Memorial Boulevard
Murfreesboro, TN 37129
(615) 893-6565
www.rutherfordchamber.org

Day Trip 2
McMinnville–Warren County Chamber of Commerce
110 South Court Square
McMinnville, TN 37110
(931) 473-6611
www.warrentn.com

Day Trip 3
Grundy County Chamber of Commerce
HCR 76, P.O. Box 578
Gruetli-Laager, TN 37339
(931) 779-3462
www.grundychamber.com

Franklin County Chamber of Commerce
P.O. Box 280
Winchester, TN 37398
(931) 967-6788
www.franklincountychamber.com

Day Trip 4
Chattanooga Area Convention and Visitors Bureau
2 Broad Street
Chattanooga, TN 37402
(800) 322-3344 or (423) 756-8687
www.chattanoogafun.com

Day Trip 5
Tennessee's Backroads Heritage
300 South Jackson Street
Tullahoma, TN 37388
(800) 799-6131 or (931) 454-9446
www.tennweb.com/tnbkrds

Shelbyville–Bedford County Chamber of Commerce
100 North Cannon Boulevard
Shelbyville, TN 37160
(931) 684-3482
www.shelbyvilletn.com

Tullahoma Chamber of Commerce
135 West Lincoln Street
Tullahoma, TN 37388
(931) 455-5497
www.tullahoma.org

SOUTH

Day Trip 1

Williamson County-Franklin Chamber of Commerce
City Hall
109 Second Avenue South
Franklin, TN 37065
(615) 794-1225
www.williamson-franklinchamber.com

Shelbyville–Bedford County Chamber of Commerce
100 North Cannon Boulevard
Shelbyville, TN 37160
(931) 684-3482
www.shelbyvilltn.com

Lynchburg Welcome Center
Mechanic Street
Lynchburg, TN 37352
(931) 759-4111
www.lynchburgtn.com

Day Trip 2

Fayetteville–Lincoln County Chamber of Commerce
208 South Elk Avenue
Fayetteville, TN 37334
(931) 433-1235
www.vallnet.com/chamberofcommerce

Huntsville–Madison County Convention and Visitors Bureau
500 Church Street
Huntsville, AL 35801
(800) SPACE4U or (256) 533–5723
www.huntsville.org

Day Trip 3
Brentwood Chamber of Commerce
5211 Maryland Way
Brentwood, TN 37027
(615) 373–1595
www.brentwood.org

Williamson County–Franklin Chamber of Commerce
and Tourism Information Center
City Hall
109 Second Avenue South
Franklin, TN 37065
(615) 794–1225
www.williamson-franklinchamber.com

Maury County Convention and Visitors Bureau/
Middle Tennessee Visitors Bureau
8 Public Square
Columbia, TN 38401
(888) 852–1860 or (931) 381–7176

SOUTHWEST

Day Trip 1
Natchez Trace Parkway
2680 Natchez Trace Parkway
Tupelo, MS 38801
(800) 305–7417 or (601) 680–4027
www.nps.gov/natr

Day Trip 2
Hickman County Chamber of Commerce
117 North Central Avenue
Centerville, TN 37033
(931) 729-5774
www.hickmanco.com/chamber.htm

Lewis County Chamber of Commerce
112 East Main Street
Hohenwald, TN 38462
(931) 796-4084
www.visitlewis.com

Lawrence County Chamber of Commerce
1609 North Locust Avenue
Lawrenceburg, TN 38464
(931) 762-4911
www.lawrenceburg.com/chamber

Day Trip 3
Hardin County Convention and Visitors Bureau
507 Main Street
Savannah, TN 38372
(800) 552-FUNN or (731) 925-2364
www.tourhardincounty.org

McNairy County Chamber of Commerce
144 West Cypress Street
Selmer, TN 38375
(731) 645-6360
www.mcnairy.com

WEST

Day Trip 1
Cheatham County Chamber of Commerce
108 South Main Street
Ashland City, TN 37015
(615) 792-6722
www.cheathamchamber.org

Dickson County Chamber of Commerce
119 TN-70E
Dickson, TN 37055
(615) 446-2349
www.dicksoncountychamber.com

Humphreys County Chamber of Commerce
124 East Main Street
Waverly, TN 37185
(931) 296-4865
www.dickson.net/hcchamber

Camden County-Benton Chamber of Commerce
202 West Main Street
Camden, TN 38320
(731) 584-8395
www.bentoncountycamden.com/chamber

Day Trip 2
Natchez Trace Information Center
Wildersville, TN 38388
(800) 250-8616 or (901) 968-3742
www.state.tn.us/environment/parks/parks/NatchezTrace

NORTHWEST

Day Trip 1
Cheatham County Chamber of Commerce
108 South Main Street
Ashland City, TN 37015
(615) 792-6722
www.cheathamchamber.org

Stewart County Chamber of Commerce
367 Spring Street
Dover, TN 37058
(931) 232-8290
www.stewartcountytn.org

Tennessee Valley Authority
Land Between the Lakes
100 Van Morgan Drive
Golden Pond, KY 42211
(800) LBL-7077 or (270) 924-2000
www.lbl.org

Cadiz-Trigg County Tourist Commission
22 Main Street
Cadiz, KY 42211
(270) 522-3892
www.gocadiz.com

Day Trip 2
Paducah-McCracken County Convention and Visitors Bureau
128 Broadway
Paducah, KY 42001
(800) PADUCAH or (270) 443-8783
www.paducah-tourism.org

Day Trip 3
Cheatham County Chamber of Commerce
108 South Main Street
Ashland City, TN 37015
(615) 792-6722
www.cheathamchamber.org

Clarksville-Montgomery County Tourist Information Center
180 Holiday Road
Clarksville, TN 37040
(931) 553-8467

Springfield-Robertson County Chamber of Commerce
100 Fifth Avenue West
Springfield, TN 37172
(615) 384-3800
www.springfieldtennchamber.org

Festivals and Celebrations

The states in the Southeast region seem to always be celebrating something—be it poke sallet or barbecue, walking horses or catfish. There's a festival to suit every interest, and most are fun-filled events with music, food, and entertainment.

For a list of Tennessee's annual events, write the Tennessee Tourist Development Office, 320 Sixth Avenue North, Rachel Jackson Building, Nashville, TN 37243; call (615) 741-2158; or visit www.state.tn.us/tourdev.

For information on Kentucky's festivals and celebrations write the Kentucky Department of Travel Development, Capital Plaza Tower, 500 Mero Street, Suite 2200, Frankfort, KY 40601; call (800) 225-TRIP or (502) 564-4930; or visit www.kentuckytourism.com.

Alabama stages its share of annual events, too. Write the Alabama Bureau of Tourism and Travel, P.O. Box 4927, Montgomery, AL 36103; call (800) ALA-BAMA or (334) 242-4644; or visit www .touralabama.org.

For information on Georgia's annual events, contact the Georgia Department of Industry, Trade, and Tourism, P.O. Box 1776, Atlanta, GA 30301; call (800) 847-4842 or (404) 656-3590; or visit www.georgia.org.

The following descriptions cover the highlights of events that take place in the travel areas covered by this book. A few of the celebrations don't appear on a day trip route but are fun events to attend.

FEBRUARY

Heart of Country Antiques Show, Gaylord Opryland Resort and Convention Center, Nashville, TN. Approximately 175 dealers show and sell antiques from all areas of the country. Furniture, fine art, folk art, and textiles as well as lectures make up the four-day festival, which is also held in October. (800) 862–1090 or (615) 889–1000; www.heartofcountry.com.

MARCH

Erin's Irish Celebration, Erin, TN. There's no better place for an Irish festival than in Erin. The small town celebrates in a big way with a parade, golf and bass tournaments, an auction, a beauty contest, a carnival and fun run, a community-wide banquet, and an Irish ball. (931) 289–5100.

My Old Kentucky Home Festival of Quilts, Bardstown, KY. This is the official quilt festival of Kentucky, with a juried exhibit of new and antique quilts from across the country. Educational workshops and a Victorian tea also take place. (800) 638–4877 or (502) 348–0255.

Tennessee Old-Time Fiddlers' Championship, Clarksville, TN. Some of the best fiddlers take part in this two-day festival, competing in more than a dozen categories for cash prizes. (931) 648–0001.

APRIL

Annual Main Street Festival, Franklin, TN. Here you can enjoy food, live entertainment, and more than 250 of the region's leading craft artists at a downtown fair. There are also games and rides for the children. (615) 591–8500.

Huntsville Pilgrimage of Homes, Huntsville, AL. Selected homes in the historic districts of Twickenham and Old Town open their doors to the public for two days in April. Related activities occur citywide. (800) SPACE4U or (256) 551–2230.

Mile Long Yard Sale, Watertown, TN. Every April in Watertown, folks stage a yard sale that stretches the length of Main Street. Items to suit every interest can be found at this "sale of sales." (615) 237–0270.

Mule Day, Columbia, TN. In early April the city celebrates its heritage in mule trading. There is a mule sale, mule pullings, a parade, arts and crafts, a flea market, an old-time fiddlers' contest, and a knife show. (931) 381–9557; www.muleday.com.

Paducah Dogwood Festival, Paducah, KY. This mid-April event spotlights the blooming dogwood tree. There is an art show, a theater production, home tours, a symphony concert, and the 12-mile lighted dogwood trail. The American Quilter's National Society Quilt Show is held at the same time. (800) PADUCAH or (270) 433–8783.

Panoply, Huntsville, AL. Both performing and visual arts are on tap at this late-April event held in Big Spring International Park. Entertainment features singers, dancers, and actors. (256) 535–6565.

World's Biggest Fish Fry, Paris, TN. More than 10,000 pounds of fish, along with hush puppies, white beans, and cole slaw, are served at this event sponsored by the Paris–Henry County Jaycees. You'll also find arts and crafts, a carnival, a rodeo, and an antique car show. (800) 345–1103 or (731) 642–3431; www.paris.tn.org.

MAY

Eighteenth-Century Colonial Fair, Goodlettsville, TN. For this fair, Historic Mansker's Station Frontier Life Center and Bowen Plantation House in Moss-Wright Park are set up with craftsmen re-creating eighteenth-century goods and others making and selling period foods. In addition to shopping for Early American merchandise, you can watch as musicians and living-history enthusiasts entertain the crowd. (615) 859–3768.

Festival of British and Appalachian Culture, Rugby, TN. Historic Rugby, Inc., sponsors this weekend event, featuring craft demonstrations and sales, British Isles and Appalachian music and dancing, and walking tours of the historic buildings. (423) 628–2441; www.historicrugby.org.

Portland Strawberry Festival, Portland, TN. A spring festival honoring the little red fruit has been held here for more than sixty years. The week of activities features a 5K run, a pancake breakfast, a parade, various foods and entertainment, and a crafts show and sale. (615) 325–9032; www.portlandtn.com.

Smiths Grove Antique Festival, Smiths Grove, KY. Antiques dealers from five states descend on this small town for wheeling and dealing; plus the town's eight antiques shops are open during the two-day fest. (270) 782-0800 or (800) 326-7465.

Tennessee Annual Poke Sallet Festival, Gainesboro, TN. The second weekend in May is a time to pay homage to poke sallet. More than one hundred booths contain arts and crafts, antiques, and quilts. There is also music, the Miss Poke Sallet Festival pageant, horse and buggy rides, odd competitions such as an outhouse race and a hay bale race, and a poke eat'n contest. (931) 268-9315.

Tennessee Renaissance Festival, Triune, TN. For four consecutive weekends, you can step back in time at the Castle Gwynn. Jousting matches, armored knights, gypsies, lute players, wandering minstrels, and other performers take center stage. Storytellers, jugglers, and games will entertain the kids, and there are arts and crafts and tours of the castle, too. (615) 395-9950 or (615) 794-1225; www.tnrenfest.com.

JUNE

Festival of Murals, Paducah, KY. This six-day event celebrates the rich history of the city with Civil War walking tours, a student essay contest, a symphony concert, and a living-history performance where characters in the downtown flood-wall murals come to life. (800) PADUCAH or (270) 443-8783.

National Corvette Homecoming, Bowling Green, KY. Corvette lovers from far and wide come together at Beech Bend Park the first weekend in June for a car show, swap meet, drag racing, and parade. Plus, a free Corvette is given away. (270) 782-0800 or (270) 448-7187.

Riverbend Festival, Chattanooga, TN. This weeklong festival features arts, children's activities, musical entertainment, and big-name concerts. The unique Bessie Smith Strut—a walk down Martin Luther King Boulevard, which is lined with food vendors and musical entertainment—also takes place. (800) 338-3999 or (423) 265-4112.

Pickin' Party, Land Between the Lakes, Golden Pond, KY. Folk and bluegrass music are center stage at this June festival, where nationally known bands play at The Homeplace-1850. (800) 525-7077; www.lbl.org.

Sewanee Music Festival, Sewanee, TN. The summer festival, which begins in June and continues through August, presents some thirty concerts open to the public. There are orchestra, chamber music, and solo concerts by students and guest artists. (931) 598-1225; www.sewanee.edu/ssmf.

Summer Shaker Festival, South Union, KY. Enjoy a weekend of Shaker food, crafts, and music on the grounds of this historic community. (800) 811-8379 or (270) 542-4167; www.shakermuseum.com.

Summertown Bluegrass Reunion, Summertown, TN. The Bluegrass Reunion brings pickers together for a weekend in June and again on Labor Day weekend, entertaining more than 3,000 fans with picking, clogging, square dancing, and buck dancing. (931) 964-2100.

JULY

Antique Show and Sale, Murfreesboro, TN. This show, on the Middle Tennessee State University campus, features more than sixty antiques and collectibles dealers from several states and is sponsored by the Murfreesboro Antique Dealers Association. (615) 895-8655.

Fiddlers' Jamboree and Crafts Festival, Smithville, TN. The weekend before Independence Day, the town square comes alive with the best of fiddlers, vying for the title of Grand Champion. Clogging, buck dancing, banjo picking, and more than 200 craft exhibitions also entertain guests. (615) 597-8500; www.smithville.com.

Folk Medicine Festival, Red Boiling Springs, TN. Learn about folk medicines and their heritage at this popular festival in Red Boiling Springs. There is also music, arts and crafts exhibits, and entertainment for the kids. (615) 699-2011; www.redboilingsprings .com or www.maconcountytennessee.com.

Kentucky Music Weekend, Bardstown, KY. This is said to be the largest traditional Kentucky music festival in the state. It features concerts, workshops, old-time street dances, and crafts. (800) 638-4877 or (502) 348-5237.

Paducah Summer Fest, Paducah, KY. This ten-day celebration centers around the Ohio River, where there is boating, hot-air balloons, bicycle races, sky divers, fireworks, arts and crafts, and nightly entertainment. The Taste of Paducah allows festival-goers to sample food from area restaurants. (800) PADUCAH or (270) 443-8783.

Savannah Bluegrass Festival, Savannah, TN. Performers play bluegrass on Friday and Saturday night here in early July, with fireworks following the shows. (800) 552-3866 or (731) 925-8181; www.tourhardincnty.org.

Sewanee Music Festival, Sewanee, TN. (See listing in June.)

St. Patrick's Day Picnic and Homecoming, McEwen, TN. It's the barbecue that brings people to McEwen, and there's plenty of it. Some 20,000 pounds of pork shoulder and 2,000 chickens all cooked in a secret barbecue sauce (said to have been brought over from Ireland and kept in the town's bank vault) are served up at this event, which has been going on for about 145 years. There is bottled sauce for sale, plus square dancing, bluegrass music, and children's games. (931) 582-3986.

Tennessee–Kentucky Threshermen's Show, Adams, TN. In mid-July, Adams is the spot for seeing antique wheat threshers, tractors, and other types of steam engines in action. Arts and crafts, a tractor and mule pull, and square dancing round out the affair. Plus storytellers spin the tale of the Bell Witch. (615) 696-2058.

Uncle Dave Macon Days, Murfreesboro, TN. This weekend festival honors Uncle Dave, one of the first stars of the Grand Ole Opry, with old-time music, dancing, arts and crafts, and a parade on the grounds of Cannonsburgh. (615) 893-2369.

Watertown Jazz Festival, Watertown, TN. The town square comes alive with jazz, local cuisine, and the warm breezes of a summer night. Bring a lawn chair and your listening ears. (615) 237-0270 or (615) 237-9999.

AUGUST

Beersheba Springs Arts and Crafts Festival, Beersheba Springs, TN. Each August, the Beersheba Springs Hotel becomes the backdrop for an arts and crafts festival featuring about 250 exhibitors from several different states, and it's the only time during the year that the hotel is open to the public. (931) 327-1533.

Bell Witch Bluegrass Festival, Adams, TN. Old and young alike come to the Old Bell School grounds to hear bluegrass music and watch musicians and dancers compete for prizes in banjo, guitar, Dobro, mandolin, harmonica, fiddle, clogging, and square dancing.

The music provides a pleasant backdrop for viewing the antiques on display inside the old school during the two-day festival. (615) 696-2589.

450 Mile Highway 127 Corridor Sale, Jamestown, TN. The "World's Longest Outdoor Sale" stretches from Covington, Kentucky, to Chattanooga, Tennessee, and then down to Gadsden, Alabama. Farm-fresh produce, crafts, antiques, handmade quilts, and country cookin' are in store for shoppers, who will wheel and deal with some 3,300 vendors. Headquarters are at the Fentress County Chamber of Commerce. (800) 327-3945; www.jamestowntn.org/worlds.htm.

Franklin Jazz Festival, Franklin, TN. Franklin's town square is the place to hear traditional jazz, Dixieland, and the big band sound, with food and beverages also on tap. (615) 791-1777.

Historic Rugby Pilgrimage of Homes, Rugby, TN. Every other August this quaint community opens up its private homes and public buildings for visitors. There is period food, dancing, and educational programs. (423) 628-2441; www.historicrugby.org.

International Grand Championship Walking Horse Show, Murfreesboro, TN. Early August brings more than 800 Tennessee walking horses to Murfreesboro, where they compete for prizes in a weeklong event, second only to the Tennessee Walking Horse National Celebration in Shelbyville, Tennessee. (615) 890-9120.

Sewanee Music Festival, Sewanee, TN. (See listing in June.)

Summertown Bluegrass Reunion, Summertown, TN. (See listing in June.)

Tennessee Walking Horse National Celebration, Shelbyville, TN. Since 1939, this ten-day event has celebrated the Tennessee walking horse. More than 2,000 horses compete for prizes and awards as well as the World Grand Champion title. (931) 684-5915; www.twhnc.com.

SEPTEMBER

Barbecue on the River and Old Market Days, Paducah, KY. Get a taste of some 'cue from some of the amateur chefs while shopping for antiques, crafts, local art, and fresh produce. Music and games round out the festival. (800) PADUCAH or (270) 443-8783.

Harvest Celebration and Annual Trades Fair, Land Between the Lakes, Golden Pond, KY. This festival, staged at The Homeplace–1850, celebrates the traditional fall harvest with activities like apple butter making, candle dipping, and sauerkraut making. In addition, there are wagon rides, storytelling, food, and demonstrations of traditional trades and crafts. (800) LBL-7077 or (270) 924-2020; www.lbl.org.

Kentucky Bourbon Festival, Bardstown, KY. Everything you ever wanted to know about bourbon can be found out at this weekend festival. Distillery tours, barbecue picnic, music, bourbon barrel relays, and a golf tournament are just a few of the activities slated for the annual event. (800) 638-4877.

Lincoln County Fair, Fayetteville, TN. This is the place to see harness racing, exhibits, animals, a rodeo, and a demolition derby and eat, play games, and visit the midway. It's been a tradition in Lincoln County for more than ninety-six years. (931) 433-1234.

Majestic Middle Tennessee Fall Tour, Columbia, TN. This end-of-September tour features more than ten historic homes and churches, most of which are on the National Register of Historic Places. Each year the tour takes guests to sites rich in historical and architectural detail. (931) 381-4822.

Old Fashioned Trade Day, Huntsville, AL. Huntsville's Courthouse Square becomes the site of an old-fashioned trade day. Booths selling crafts, antiques, food, and other merchandise line the streets. (800) SPACE4U or (256) 883-9446.

Quilt Walk, Bell Buckle, TN. This quilt exhibition and home tour is held the third Saturday in September. Demonstrations, seminars, food, and a fashion show round out the popular event. (931) 684-3482; www.bellbucklechamber.com/events.

Rolling Fork Iron Horse Festival, New Haven, KY. Train rides and stage shows bring people in for this two-day celebration. There is also a parade, street dancing, arts and crafts, a classic car display, animal-calling contests, and old-time demonstrations. (502) 549-3177.

Summertown Bluegrass Reunion, Summertown, TN. (See listing in June.)

Watertown Hoedown, Watertown, TN. The whole town comes out in mid-September to browse arts and crafts booths, hear live music, eat, and shuffle around the square at the evening dance. (615) 237-0270.

OCTOBER

Fall Color Cruise and Folk Festival, Chattanooga, TN. One of the largest boating events in the South brings cruisers to enjoy the fall foliage, arts and crafts, and a folk festival. (800) 338–3999 or (423) 892–0223.

Fall Mile Long Yard Sale, Watertown, TN. Every October in Watertown, folks stage a yard sale that stretches the length of Main Street. Items to suit every interest can be found at this "sale of sales." (615) 237–0270.

Ghostly Gatherings, Rugby, TN. Historic Rugby offers candle and lantern tours in the evenings, and entertaining stories at this time of year. (423) 628–2441; www.historicrugby.org.

Glendale Crossing Festival, Glendale, KY. More than 250 arts and crafts booths, a parade, entertainment, food, games, a Halloween costume contest, and an antique farm machinery show make this small town a hot spot during the third Saturday in October. (270) 369–6188.

Heart of Country Antiques Show, Gaylord Opryland Hotel, Nashville, TN. (See listing in February.)

Great Pumpkin Festival, Allardt, TN. Family activities abound at this festival, which is usually held in early October. There's a parade, a weigh-off of pumpkins, and a "Tallest Cornstalk" contest. (931) 879–7125.

Jack Daniel's World Championship Invitational Barbecue, Lynchburg, TN. This October celebration in Jack Daniel's country is for barbecue lovers. Teams cook up whole hog, pork shoulder, pork ribs, beef, and poultry, competing for the World Champion title. (931) 759–4221.

Lincoln Days Celebration, Hodgenville, KY. Celebrants commemorate the former president's birth with a parade, pioneer games, craft demonstrations, and a Lincoln look-alike contest during the second weekend of October. (270) 358–3411.

Meriwether Lewis Arts & Crafts Fair, Natchez Trace Parkway (near Hohenwald, TN). This annual event, which takes place the second full weekend in October, features pottery, jewelry, wooden toys, and leather goods and honors famed explorer Meriwether

Lewis, who met his untimely death on the parkway in 1809. (800) 305-7417 or (601) 680-4025.

Smith County Fall Heritage Festival, Carthage, TN. This early October festival entertains visitors with handmade crafts and demonstrations, wagon rides, storytellers, antique tractors, and live music and dancing. (615) 735-9430.

Smiths Grove Antique Festival, Smiths Grove, KY. (See listing in May.)

Tennessee Highland Games, Murfreesboro, TN. Early October brings together clans with a variety of competitions, ranging from drumming and highland dancing to traditional Scottish athletics. Entertainment, demonstrations, and children's activities round out the three-day event, which is held at Middle Tennessee State University. (615) 848-9193.

Tobacco Festival, Russellville, KY. The second week in October is a time to celebrate this small Kentucky town's main cash crop. Parades, pageants, a walk/run, arts and crafts, entertainment, and a tobacco judging contest draw visitors from all over. (270) 726-2206.

Trigg County Ham Festival, Cadiz, KY. This Kentucky festival, held the second weekend of October, celebrates the Broadbent ham, which has been raised, processed, and cured in Trigg County for three generations. The celebration features arts and crafts, entertainment, and consumption of what is considered the world's largest ham biscuit. (270) 522-3892.

Webb School Arts and Crafts Festival, Bell Buckle, TN. Webb School hosts Bell Buckle's arts and crafts fair each October, showcasing the best in handmade collectibles. (931) 684-3482.

NOVEMBER

Christmas at Trinity Music City, USA, Hendersonville, TN. This holiday fantasy world enchants both young and old with a million twinkling lights and special performances on thirty acres of beautifully decorated grounds. Life-size nativity scenes, strolling carolers, and Christmas shopping make a visit worthwhile. (615) 826-9191.

A Country Christmas, Gaylord Opryland Resort and Convention Center, Nashville, TN. Musical stage shows, a yule log ceremony, and crafts and antiques all become part of the magic at the hotel during this time of year. (615) 889–1000.

Fayetteville . . . Host of Christmas Past, Fayetteville, TN. Get in the spirit the second Saturday and Sunday in November by sharing the Christmas holiday with this small town. Trolley rides, high tea, candlelit walking tours, carolers, live reindeer, and, of course, Santa himself make this a fun tradition. (931) 433–1234.

DECEMBER

Carter House Candlelight Tour of Homes, Franklin, TN. Several historic homes—including the Carter House—are decorated in their Christmas finery and on tour the first weekend in December, with musical entertainment. (615) 791–1861; www.carter-house.org.

Christmas at Rugby, Rugby, TN. During two Saturdays in December, visitors can tour candlelit historic buildings, hear classical music, see some of Rugby's early settlers portrayed by professional actors, attend a special service at Christ Church Episcopal, and have a sumptuous Victorian dinner at the Harrow Road Cafe. (423) 628–2441; www.historicrugby.org.

Christmas in Lynchburg, Lynchburg, TN. In early December, strolling carolers, storytelling, wagon rides, a Christmas parade, and a lighting ceremony start the season off right in historic Lynchburg. (931) 759–4111.

Christmas on the River, Chattanooga, TN. Ross's Landing is where the decorated boats come to share the holiday in early December. Area groups carol, and there is a fireworks display at the end of the day. (423) 265–0771; www.chattanoogafun.com.

Dickens of a Christmas, Franklin, TN. Christmas carolers in Victorian costumes, strolling characters from *A Christmas Carol,* a theater production, hot wassail, and a horse-drawn carriage help create a Dickensian atmosphere here. Downtown Franklin restaurants feature nineteenth-century dishes and tea-time treats. (615) 591–8500.

State and National Parks

The Tennessee parks system consists of fifty-four state parks, ranging from those centered around the water, such as Paris Landing on Kentucky Lake, to those suited for golfers, such as Henry Horton or Montgomery Bell. Fall Creek Falls Resort Park in southeastern Tennessee boasts the highest waterfall east of the Rocky Mountains, and Nathan Bedford Forrest Historical Area in western Tennessee is home to the Tennessee River Folklife Center, which explores the relationship between the river and the people who use it.

There's a frisbee golf course at Cedars of Lebanon Recreational Park, which is the largest remaining red cedar forest in the nation, and the Narrows of the Harpeth State Historic Area displays a one-hundred-yard tunnel chiseled through solid rock—the remains of the early 1880s industrial complex that was located there.

The majority of parks have campsites, and there are some lovely resort inns and modern cabins located across the state in which to bed down, too. Tennessee's rivers and lakes provide popular fishing and water recreation—from waterskiing to houseboating. Anglers will find crappie, bluegill, white bass, catfish, yellow bass, yellow perch, and walleye, among other species in Tennessee's waters. Hunting in the state is something generations of residents have enjoyed, with small game, deer, and waterfowl plentiful.

Tennessee requires fishing and hunting licenses. More information about regulations in the state is available from the Tennessee Wildlife Resources Agency, P.O. Box 40747, Nashville, TN 37204; (615) 781-6622.

The state parks stage numerous events throughout the year. Bike-a-thons, fishing tournaments, gospel music festivals, boat cruises, and other interesting programs are offered. Program services can be reached at (615) 532-0016.

For more information on the parks system, write Tennessee State Parks, 401 Church Street, 7th floor L&C Tower, Nashville, TN 37243; call (800) 421-6683 (in-state) or (615) 532-0001; or visit www.tnstateparks.com.

KENTUCKY

Kentucky has fifty resort parks, recreation parks, and historic sites, some of which are described in this book. Most of them have campsites, and some have primitive camping available. Travelers who prefer sleeping in a bed will enjoy the lodges and cottages available at many of the state's parks and resorts.

Like Tennessee, Kentucky is a haven for fishermen, hunters, and those who enjoy the outdoors. Deer, wild turkey, and Canada geese are all fair game. A valid Kentucky hunting license is a must. The state also has seventy-three public wildlife areas. For more information, write the Kentucky Department of Fish and Wildlife Resources, #1 Game Farm Road, Frankfort, KY 40601; or call (502) 564-4336.

Canoeing, boating, and rafting are all popular activities in the state. Most of Kentucky's parks host special events throughout the year, and at many of them you'll find naturalists and recreation leaders who oversee activities for both children and adults. The state park system spent about $70 million to revitalize some of the properties and programs. To get more material on the Bluegrass State's parks, contact the Kentucky Department of Parks, 500 Mero Street, 11th Floor, Frankfort, KY 40601; (800) 255-PARK or (502) 564-2172. There is a toll-free travel information number as well: (800) 225-TRIP; or you can visit http://parks.ky.gov.

ALABAMA

Alabama has twenty-four state parks, six of which have lodges and convention facilities. Outdoor enthusiasts will find camping, cabins, water recreation activities, and special events scheduled throughout the year. Hunting and fishing are both popular in Alabama, and a license is required for both. For more information, contact the Game and Fish Division, 64 North Union Street, Montgomery, AL 36130; (334) 242–3465. For general park information, write to the Alabama State Parks Division, 64 North Union Street, Montgomery, AL 36130; call (800) ALA–PARK or (334) 242–3333; or visit www.alapark.com.

GEORGIA

While Georgia also has a wealth of state parks, the only day trip that extends into the state is the trip to the Chattanooga area.

The Chickamauga and Chattanooga National Military Park in Fort Oglethorpe, Georgia, and Chattanooga is part of the national park system. For more information about Georgia's sixty-three state parks and historic sites, write to Georgia State Parks, 205 Butler Street, S.E., Atlanta, GA 30334; or call (800) 864–7275 or (404) 656–3530; or visit www.gastateparks.org.

NATIONAL PARKS

The Big South Fork National River and Recreation area stretches from Tennessee into Kentucky, and there are several national battlefields located in Tennessee. Kentucky has six nationally designated outdoor recreation areas/historic sites, including Land Between the Lakes and Mammoth Cave National Park. Alabama has five national forests within its borders. In addition, the Natchez Trace Parkway is maintained by the National Park Service. For more information on these nationally designated areas, contact the individual attractions.

Guide to Southern Cuisine

From barbecue and country ham to turnip greens and fried okra, peach cobbler and pecan pie, Southern food is hearty and comforting. While perhaps not the most healthful cuisine—with ingredients such as lard and fatback—it's tasty and warms the soul. Many trendy restaurants have taken traditional Southern ingredients and concocted more healthful entrees, providing the best of both worlds. Still, from the tiniest cafe to the largest buffet, the dishes are basically the same everywhere. Fried chicken, hush puppies, congealed salad, corn bread, and macaroni and cheese appear on most menus, along with other traditional favorites such as butter beans, country ham, yams, and cheese grits.

And a Southern meal wouldn't be the same without biscuits and iced tea. Nothing beats made-from-scratch biscuits served warm with either red-eye or milk gravy or with a slab of butter and some homemade preserves. Iced tea is served in volumes. "Sweet tea" is generally loaded with sugar but is a satisfactory thirst-quencher for the masses of sweet-toothed Southerners.

Then there is chess pie. The story goes that when someone once asked a cook what kind of pie she was making, she announced, "It's jes' pie," and so it was named. The sweet custard is quite a treat.

Barbecue in Tennessee differs from that in other parts of the country because here it always comes from a pig. While you can find barbecue beef at some eateries, you'd do better to order up a pork shoulder plate or some ribs. In Western Kentucky, you can find mutton on the menu, though.

"Meat-and-threes" are simply restaurants that offer plate lunches. That usually translates to one meat—be it a pork chop, fried chicken, or meatloaf—served with a choice of three vegetables (from a selection of a dozen or more), most often accompanied by a couple of biscuits or corn bread. Top it off with some tea and dessert, and you'll have had a meal in fine Southern tradition.

ABOUT THE AUTHOR

Susan Chappell has been a book, magazine, newspaper, and newsletter editor and writer since 1980. She is also the author of *Nashville Inside Out,* published by Two Lane Press of Kansas City, and *The Opryland Insider's Guide to Nashville,* published by the Ballantine Publishing Group in New York. She is currently senior editor at Journal Communications Inc., and lives with her family in Nashville.